63-3986 (9-19-47)

URUGUAY

URUGUAY

by

GEORGE PENDLE

Third Edition

Issued under the auspices of the
Royal Institute of International Affairs

OXFORD UNIVERSITY PRESS
LONDON NEW YORK TORONTO

Oxford University Press, Amen House, London, E.C.4

GLASGOW NEW YORK TORONTO MELBOURNE WELLINGTON
BOMBAY CALCUTTA MADRAS KARACHI LAHORE DACCA
CAPE TOWN SALISBURY NAIROBI IBADAN ACCRA
KUALA LUMPUR HONG KONG

First edition 1952
Second edition 1957
Third edition 1963
Reprinted (with corrections) 1965

Printed in Great Britain by
Latimer Trend & Co. Ltd., Plymouth and Whitstable

PREFACE TO THIRD EDITION

I AM indebted to B.O.A.C. for enabling me to re-visit Uruguay since the second edition of this book was published. I have known Uruguay for more than thirty years, in good times and bad—that is to say, when the world price of wool (the chief product) was high, and when it was low. On the last occasion, times were particularly bad. The price of wool had fallen, and the meat-packing plants were operating for only about half of the year. Walking along the streets of central Montevideo I could feel—or I imagined that I felt—that there had been a decline in prosperity. It seemed that many of the people were not quite so well dressed as before. Buildings looked rather shabby. I was told that the payment of old-age pensions was being made with even greater delays than usual—and this in a country that had such a fine record of social-welfare legislation.

But then, with the beginning of the summer season, crowds of holiday-makers arrived from Argentina. The streets of Montevideo became as animated as I had ever known them to be in the past. Outside town, up the sandy coasts that stretch to Punta del Este and beyond, hotels and chalets were gay in the sunlight. And the foreign currency that the tourists brought into Uruguay reduced the nation's deficit by about one third.

The foreigner should not take too seriously the Uruguayans' disparagements of their homeland. They have no great national ambitions—except at football. They have accepted the fact that their country is not destined to be a major world power.[1] Their patriotism takes the form of modest pride that they are *not* involved in the struggle for power and that other

---

[1] An Uruguayan has written of his countrymen: 'The Uruguayan does not wish to be a very important man, or an insignificant one. He just wants to live in freedom, without making any great sacrifices, and without forcing others to make them. Here is a country whose people do not aspire to greatness, or to anything absolute, but who desire that things shall be kept in good, human proportion and that the human values shall be treated with proper respect. With such a people one does not build empires or alter the course of history. Here, nothing is very rigorous. Everything is improvised, haphazard and rather ineffectual. In the end, everything is settled by conversation, and never completely' (Carlos Maggi in *Marcha*, Montevideo, 24 November 1961).

nations respect them for their faith in international co-opera-
tion. In the last century Uruguay came to be recognized as a
natural and indispensable buffer state. Nowadays Montevideo and Punta del Este are looked upon as natural places for
the delegates of such bodies as the Organization of American
States and the Latin American Free Trade Area to meet together to discuss their differences. Perhaps the consciousness
that they really are *needed* provides the explanation of the
Uruguayans' ability to treat their country's problems light-
heartedly.

For help in the preparation of this edition I thank Roberto
Zabaleta, Hugh A. Holley, and Miss M. B. James. I am grate-
ful to the Bank of London and South America, who supplied
many of the statistics.

G. P.

NOTE TO THE PRESENT REPRINT

This book, like my affection for Uruguay, has developed
with the years; a few further improvements have now been
made to the text.

I thank Mario Benedeti, the distinguished Uruguayan
novelist, for the delightful article about the third edition,
'Un Inglés nos mira: Pendle exámina al Uruguay objetiva-
mente', which appeared in the Montevideo daily newspaper *La Mañana*, on 21 March 1963.

CONTENTS

Chapter I

THE LAND

AN isolated, cone-shaped hill rises upon the northern shore of the Río de la Plata estuary. For the early mariners, this hill on the otherwise flat coastline was a well-known and a welcome landmark, and although its summit is less than 500 feet above sea-level, they referred to it as 'the mountain'. In 1688 the buccaneer-surgeon Lionel Wafer and his companions, after a terrible voyage in the South Atlantic,

> put ashore here to get Water and fresh Provisions, of which this Country afforded plenty: And here our Men having with them their Fusees, spy'd a Herd of Sea-Swine, as we call them, upon a Point of Land; and were thereupon resolved to kill some of them to bring on board. In order thereunto they contrived, that some Men should stop the Pass that led up to the Mountain, whilst others went in among them, and with their Cutlasses did what Execution they could. But still as the Men came near them, the Herd walked toward the Sea, contrary to our Mens expectation; for they hither-to took them to be Land-Swine. There they stood on the Shore, staring at and admiring our People: but when the Men came near enough, and were just going to strike among them, the whole Herd jump'd into the Sea, leaving the Men in amazement.[1]

At that time, the country was uninhabited; but today Uruguay's capital city, Montevideo, lies at the base of 'the mountain', which is now known as the Cerro. Wafer's 'Sea-Swine' of course were sea-lions; and sea-lions still frequent these waters.[2]

Uruguay is the smallest of the South American republics.[3] It occupies a region where the warm uplands of southern Brazil extend to meet the flat expanse of the temperate Argentine pampa. It is an abundantly watered land. From the rounded, inland hills, streams flow eastwards into the lagoons that lie

[1] Lionel Wafer, *A New Voyage and Description of the Isthmus of America*, ed. L. E. Elliott Joyce (Oxford, Hakluyt Society, 1934), p. 129.
[2] See below, p. 64.
[3] The area of Uruguay is about 72,150 square miles.

behind the sandy beaches and dunes of the Atlantic coast, or find their way by small estuaries to the ocean itself. On the farther, western side of the watershed, longer rivers descend through narrow valleys to join the great Río Uruguay, which forms the frontier with Argentina. The biggest of these tributaries is the Río Negro, which crosses the country diagonally from north-east to south-west, providing in its course hydro-electric power for a large area of the republic.

The country takes its name from the Río Uruguay. The word probably means 'the river of shell-fish', being derived from the ancient Guaraní-Indian *uruguä*, which is a species of mussel, called *caracol del agua* in Spanish. Another possible explanation is that the name of the river signifies 'the water where the *urú* birds come from', the Guaraní components being *urú* (the name of the birds), *gua* (to proceed from), and *y* (water).[4] In either case, the title of the republic is appropriate to a land of rivers, lagoons, and well-watered pastures.

The hills from which the streams descend are of granite, and along certain of their ridges grey rocks break through the surface soil, creating an angular outline and justifying the local appellation of *sierra* or *cuchilla*. To tourists from the Argentine pampa who visit Uruguay in summer,[5] the hills seem truly alpine, though their highest points are not more than 2,000 feet above sea-level and most of their high ridges are only of about the same altitude as the top of New York's Empire State building.

Towards the west—between the central belt of hilly ground and the Río Uruguay—the land gradually opens out into flood-plains of the kind that are characteristic of the whole Río de la Plata basin. The Río Uruguay is navigable by steamers of 14 feet draught as far as the town of Paysandú. Thereafter, it is interrupted by rapids, the biggest falls being at Salto, which is destined to become Uruguay's second chief hydro-electric centre. There is also a project for constructing a canal which will by-pass the Salto rapids and thus enable navigation to proceed much farther north, towards the interior of Brazil.

---

[4] The author is indebted to León Cadogan for this interpretation.
[5] See below, pp. 56–57.

As for the coastline: a belt of sandy lowland extends southwards down the Atlantic seaboard from the Brazilian frontier to the Río de la Plata estuary. Many ships, seeking the estuary, have gone ashore on this coast. In addition to the natural hazards, the people of the department of Maldonado used to make a practice of tying lights to the horns of their cows to lure seamen to destruction—until in 1874 H.M.S. *Cracker* threatened to fire on them as pirates.[6]

This is a region of violent storms—known as *pamperos*—which occur when cool winds from the southern pampas meet the warm air from the tropical north. In 1832 Charles Darwin had a memorable experience. It was a dark, stormy night.

We were surrounded [he wrote] by numerous seals and penguins, which made such strange noises, that the officer on watch reported he could hear the cattle bellowing on shore. On a second night we witnessed a splendid scene of natural fireworks; the masthead and yard-arm-ends shone with St. Elmo's light; and the form of the vane could almost be traced, as if it had been rubbed with phosphorus. The sea was so highly luminous, that the tracks of the penguins were marked by a fiery wake, and the darkness of the sky was momentarily illuminated by the most vivid lightning.[7]

At Maldonado the coastline turns inland—that is to say, westwards—to become the northern, and deeper, shore of the Río de la Plata. The town of Montevideo, with its Cerro, is situated near this coastal corner overlooking the vast area where the waters of the brown river and the ocean mingle. Montevideo is, in effect, an exterior port of call, by contrast with the three large Argentine ports (La Plata, Buenos Aires, and Rosario), all of which are upstream.

Uruguay, filling the intermediate zone between the warm plateaux of Brazil and the humid Argentine pampa, has many of the qualities of each of those regions. Most of the country was originally covered with a tall prairie-grass, similar to the native grass of the Argentine pampa; but in certain parts—in the vicinity of Rocha, for instance—palm-trees are dotted over

---

[6] M. G. and E. T. Mulhall, *Handbook of the River Plate*, 6th edition (Buenos Aires, Mulhall, 1892), p. 634.
[7] Charles Darwin, *The Voyage of the Beagle*, first published 1839, Chapter III.

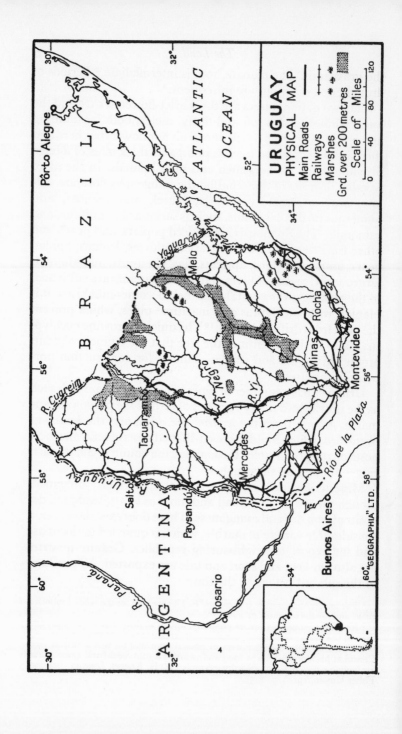

the grasslands. The climate, too, is intermediate.[8] Periods of drought do occur, but are infrequent.[9]

The two national trees are the scarlet-flowered *ceibo* and the *ombú*, whose wood is soft and fluffy, useless both for building and as fuel. The *ombú* has neither fruit nor flower, but here and there in the otherwise treeless pampa its thick mass of foliage provides shade for horsemen and their animals. In the more wooded districts of the republic the indigenous flora are willow, acacia, rosemary, myrtle, laurel, and mimosa, and numerous medicinal plants, such as sarsaparilla, quinine, and camomile. The Spaniards introduced poplars, and peach and other fruit-trees; and today grapes, oranges, lemons, apples, pears, quinces, melons, apricots, figs, chestnuts, and almonds all grow in Uruguay. Olives, dates, and bananas are cultivated in the north. As the coastal sand-belt becomes inhabited, it is planted with eucalyptus and maritime pines, which prevent the sand from drifting inland.[10] The quickly-growing eucalyptus is also (as in Argentina) the tree that the estanciero plants around his house and stables. Timber for construction purposes is imported.

Uruguay has a number of types of fur-bearing animal, such as the nutria, and many varieties of bird of the pampa and the marsh, among them the *terutero*, the *chajá*, and the *hornero* or oven-bird, which builds its oven-shaped nests of mud on fence-posts or telegraph-poles throughout the country. Small partridges abound on the ranches.

Mineral wealth is not so great as was formerly imagined, though there are some small and more or less unexploited deposits of iron ore and manganese. There does exist, however, a considerable variety of marble, which is quarried for local use and for export to neighbouring republics. Granite quarries are also worked, and sand and talc are exported. All products of the sub-soil belong to the state.

---

[8] The lowest temperature is about 35°F. The average for the coldest month is 50°F. and for the warmest 72°F.

[9] Rainfall averages 43 inches annually, and is slightly heavier in the north than in the south; but there is considerable irregularity from year to year.

[10] The originator of this system of coastal afforestation was a British Vice-Consul at Maldonado who in 1909 was awarded a gold medal and 3,000 dollars for having set such a praiseworthy example (W. H. Koebel, *Uruguay* (London, Fisher Unwin, 1911), p. 203).

Chapter II

THE PEOPLE

THE Uruguayan countryside has an air of freshness, and this same quality is felt in the towns. Even in Montevideo,[1] the air of country and river comes into the streets. Atlantic breezes, too, blow through the capital; but it is a remarkable fact that, although the republic has such an extensive seaboard and occupies such a strategic position upon one of the world's great maritime highways, the Uruguayans are not a seafaring people but are orientated towards the interior of their land, towards the pastures and the rivers. 'Uruguay', wrote Lord Bryce, who visited South America in 1910, 'has neither mountains, nor deserts, nor antiquities, nor aboriginal Indians. . . . It is a cheerful country, with scenery constructed, so to speak, on a small scale, as befits a small republic.'[2] And that summary is exact.

The inhabitants of Uruguay, unlike those of many other South American nations, are almost wholly of European descent. Immigrants came principally from Spain and Italy, though small numbers also arrived from other parts of Europe, and from the Near East—for example, there is a considerable Lebanese community, engaged particularly in the textile trade. Among rural families in the outlying districts, traces of Indian ancestry are still apparent; but this mestizo class is estimated to constitute no more than 10 per cent. of the population. There are very few negroes. The total population amounts to nearly 3 million.[3]

Formerly, of course, immigration contributed substantially to the growth of the population. Nevertheless, it is calculated that between 1836 and 1926 only 648,000 immigrants arrived

[1] The population of Montevideo is about 900,000.
[2] James Bryce, *South America, Observations and Impressions* (New York, Macmillan, 1912), pp. 349 and 351.
[3] The corresponding figures for the neighbouring republics are approximately, Argentina, 21 million; Brazil, 73 million.

in Uruguay. This is not a large figure, by South American standards. Successive Governments offered inducements; but during the nineteenth century immigrants were discouraged by the disturbed state of the country. An Englishman, J. A. Beaumont, who in 1826 travelled on horseback through the riverside districts, described the desolation. The Portuguese from Brazil were then in occupation of Montevideo,[4] and Beaumont, when leaving the town, had to pass through their defences—which he reported to be 'two soldiers perched on the branches of a tree'. Next, he passed through the lines of the Uruguayan patriots, who were besieging the town. He spent the first night in a miserable *rancho*, where the meat for his supper was roasted over a wood fire on the bare earth floor in the middle of the room and the only seats were the skeletons of horses' and bullocks' heads. 'The fire-wood crackled, and the fat hissed; and the light flickered on the ghastly skulls.' On the following night Beaumont and his small party, peering in the darkness, suddenly found themselves within 150 yards of a division of the patriot army. 'Eight or ten of the men were mounted, and the rest, to the number of two hundred, were lying on the ground wrapt in their *ponchos*, and their horses grazing by their sides.' In general, however, the land was deserted. The vast herds of cattle and horses—descendants of the animals that the Spaniards had introduced two centuries before—had been driven away or slaughtered by the rival armies; and for days at a time Beaumont saw no living creatures, except a few wild ostriches and deer.

Twenty years since millions of oxen and horses covered the face of this country; but so desolate has it become that in our whole march we saw but two small herds of mares, and none of horned cattle. The buildings of various *estancias*, each of which formerly boasted of its hundred thousand head of cattle, were now forlorn and deserted, and falling to decay, or inhabited only by a few idle *peons*. These were some of the effects of the wars and insecurity of property which have afflicted this fine province.[5]

Whereas after 1852 conditions in Argentina became more

---

[4] See below, p. 23.
[5] J. A. B. Beaumont, *Travels in Buenos Ayres and the Adjacent Country* (London, Ridgeway, 1828), pp. 137, 139, 143, 145, and 150.

settled, revolutions and wars continued in Uruguay. Many
immigrants who came to the country during the second half of
the nineteenth century moved to Argentina when revolutions
broke out, or because there was more land available and richer
soil for agriculture on the other side of the Río de la Plata. Between 1879 and 1903 the average net immigration was only
4,000 a year. In the first two decades of the twentieth century,
however, conditions in Uruguay were suddenly transformed:
civil strife ended, and a number of advanced social reforms
were instituted, with the result that between 1900 and 1930
the annual net immigration rose to 15,000. In 1932, because of
the economic depression, restrictions were imposed on immigration, and after the Second World War the only immigrants permitted were farmers and skilled workmen who had
contracts of employment, and a few categories of persons with
special qualifications.

The Argentines are apt to look upon the Uruguayans as pro-
vincials, and many Uruguayans, in spite of their national
pride, are dazzled by the wealth and power of Buenos Aires.
Indeed, the country's official title is still 'República Oriental
del Uruguay', the word 'oriental' having been preserved from
the times of the Spanish Vice-Royalty of the Plata, when the
territory that is now Uruguay was known merely as the left, or
oriental, bank of the river: the Banda Oriental. Even today,
Uruguayans are often referred to as Orientales. Of the Oriental Lord Bryce remarked:

He has retained something of the breezy recklessness and audacity, the frankness and free-handedness, of the older days. A
touch of this Gaucho quality, in a milder form, is felt through all
classes of Uruguayan society. Democratic equality in manners is
combined with a high sense of personal dignity, an immense hope-
fulness, an impulsive readiness to try all experiments, a national
consciousness none the less intense because it already rejoices over
the triumphs it is going to achieve. Whether there is more of
'ideality' than in Argentina I will not venture to say, but there is
less wealth and less ostentation.[6]

[6] *South America*, pp. 356-7.

Even during the latter years of disorder, W. H. Hudson noted the simple, democratic character of the people. Hudson wrote:

It is the perfect republic: the sense of emancipation experienced in it by the wanderer from the Old World is indescribably sweet and novel. . . . I fancy I hear some wise person exclaiming, 'No, no, no! In name only is your Purple Land a republic; its constitution is a piece of waste paper, its government an oligarchy tempered by assassination and revolution.' True; but the knot of ambitious rulers all striving to pluck each other down have no power to make the people miserable. The unwritten constitution, mightier than the written one, is in the heart of every man to make him still a republican and free with a freedom it would be hard to match anywhere else on the globe.[7]

The language of Uruguay is Spanish; but, as in Argentina, there are local modifications. For example, the Spanish verb for 'to ride a horse' is *cabalgar*; but the Uruguayans use the verb *jinetear*, meaning either 'to tame wild horses by riding them' or 'to ride on horseback, publicly, with ostentation'. The rider's whip in Spanish is a *latigo*, but the Uruguayan refers to it as a *rebenque*, which was originally a rope for flogging slaves, or a ratlin. In Spain a gentleman is addressed as *Señor Don* Fulano de Tal, but in Uruguay (and elsewhere in Spanish-speaking South America) in written communications the 'Don' is omitted, and every man is briefly 'Señor'. The principal external influence on the language has come from Italy. The normal farewell, for instance, is 'Chao!' and even the Spanish 'Adiós!' has become 'Addío!' In general the language of Spain has been softened in Uruguay, thus conforming to the character of the people.

Unlike the other South American countries, Uruguay is now populated—though unevenly—throughout the full extent of its territory. The more remote districts, which are mainly pastoral, are sparsely inhabited; but there are no big territorial gaps to fill. The density of the population is about 15·21 per square kilometre, the corresponding figures for

[7] *The Purple Land*, Chapter XXVIII. This partly autobiographical novel was first published in 1885.

Argentina and Brazil being 7·2 and 8·3 respectively. According to the 1963 census, 46·43 per cent of the population is congregated in the south-eastern corner of the republic, in and around Montevideo; and this is an agricultural district. Immigrants from Europe were largely responsible for initiating the cultivation in the neighbourhood of the capital, while the descendants of the original settlers—who came from Buenos Aires—have continued to be occupied with pastoral activities. Today in the agricultural belt along the Río de la Plata there are from 65 to 125 inhabitants per square mile.

Uruguay has no large urban communities except in Montevideo. Even the livestock centres of Paysandú and Salto have only about 60,000 inhabitants each, and the meat-packing town of Fray Bentos has no more than 20,000.

Chapter III

UNDER SPANISH AND BRITISH RULE

In the early colonial period the Spaniards at Buenos Aires were principally interested in their traffic with Peru, and the overland route to Peru was remote from the Banda Oriental. During the sixteenth century, therefore, only a few small Spanish expeditions landed on the 'Oriental' shore, and these were quickly expelled or massacred by the Charrúa Indians who at that time inhabited the district. The earliest contribution to future settlement was made in about 1603, when Hernando Arias[1] of Paraguay—the first *criollo* (i.e. locally-born) Governor in the Plata, and a man of remarkable foresight—shipped 100 head of cattle and 100 horses and mares downstream to the Banda, leaving them to run wild and multiply. A few years later the first Franciscan missionaries arrived and converted to Christianity some of the less hostile Indians, while the Jesuits established a number of missions in the north.

In the course of the seventeenth century the herds introduced by Hernando Arias increased prolifically, and attracted gauchos from Buenos Aires who crossed the river to kill the cattle and collect their hides. These gauchos were nomads, with no desire to own land; but gradually, to facilitate the trade in hides, merchants from Buenos Aires settled at various points on the Uruguayan side of the estuary. Each settlement was known by the name of the merchant to whom it belonged, and many a modern Uruguayan town bears the name of the cattle-buyer who was its founder. Business expanded, so the cattle-buyers employed herders and set up headquarters in the interior.

Thus the Spaniards of Buenos Aires, although they had not officially established themselves on the Banda Oriental, already had considerable interests in the region by 1680. In that year a Portuguese expedition arrived in the Río de la Plata and erected an encampment at Colonia on the Uruguayan

[1] Known popularly in Uruguay as Hernandarias.

shore, immediately opposite Buenos Aires. The Spaniards were now obliged to take action, not only for military reasons, but also to protect the valuable hide trade, and because of the fear that the intruders would encourage the development of the contraband traffic which already existed in the Plata, to the detriment of Spain's authority and economy.[2] The Governor of Buenos Aires therefore sent an expedition against Colonia, and defeated the Portuguese; but that was only the beginning of a struggle which was to continue for nearly 200 years between Spanish-speaking settlers in the Plata and the Portuguese from Brazil. In 1726 the Spaniards built a fortress at the point where the town of Montevideo later grew up.

During the eighteenth century, as more and more land in the Banda was occupied by cattlemen from Buenos Aires, it became necessary to fix boundaries, and in this way the great estancias came into existence. Landownership spread farther and farther northwards from the river shores where it had begun. Small trading villages arose at the junctions of roads leading to and from the larger estancias and mercantile centres. All the principal roads converged upon the port of Montevideo.

The basic permanent pattern of settlement in Uruguay was thus decided (*a*) by the setting up of outposts by the cattlemen who arrived in search of the wealth with which Hernando Arias had endowed the country, and (*b*) by the determination of the Spaniards of Buenos Aires to prevent the Portuguese from pushing Brazil's frontier southwards to the banks of the Río de la Plata.

At the end of the eighteenth century Spanish power was fast declining. In 1796 Spain was again at war with England, whose control of the seas now interfered with communication between the mother country and her far-away South American dominions. At Montevideo Madrid's authority had noticeably weakened, and as a result of the arrival of non-Spanish ships and seamen the local people acquired a broader view of the world. The unexpected arrival of two English ships, in par-

---

[2] For Spanish-Portuguese rivalry for the possession of Colonia see Mario Rodríguez, 'The Genesis of Economic Attitudes in the Río de la Plata', *Hispanic American Historical Review*, May 1956, pp. 185–9.

ticular, aroused interest and speculation. The first of these two ships was the *Lady Shore*, which had sailed from Falmouth in 1797 with a cargo of female convicts destined for Botany Bay and a detachment of recruits for the New South Wales Corps. Off the coast of Brazil the soldiers, who were a motley crowd, mutinied, and murdered the captain. They then took the ship to Montevideo, where many of the women seem to have settled quite happily in burghers' homes. The second ship was the *Duff*, owned by the London Missionary Society and carrying a complement of missionaries, with their wives and children. The *Duff* set sail from Portsmouth for the South Sea Islands in 1798. Off the Brazilian coast this vessel was seized by a French privateer and was then conducted, likewise, to Montevideo. An unforeseen meeting of British saints and sinners thus took place on the banks of the Río de la Plata, 5,500 miles from home; and awkward incidents occurred. The missionaries refused to allow the women from the *Lady Shore* to converse with their wives, and were shocked by the popish practices that they observed around them. But although they had expected to be imprisoned as enemy subjects and Protestants, they were allotted comfortable dwellings for their families and received the kindest treatment. When the wife of one of the missionaries gave birth to a son, the child's baptism was attended by the captain of the French privateer and several Spaniards or *criollos*, who brought to the banquet a supply of poultry, tongues, and tarts, and a large quantity of wine. Reading the missionaries' diaries, we gain the impression that the people of Montevideo, after their long and strict supervision by Spain, were very willing to relax in the company of visitors from other lands.[3]

But the modern history of Uruguay did not properly begin until a few years later, when a series of British military and naval expeditions against the Río de la Plata revealed to the *criollos* of Buenos Aires and Montevideo that Spain was unable

---

[3] The diaries are: (i) William Howell, *Some Interesting Particulars of the Second Voyage made by the Missionary Ship, the 'Duff'* . . . (Knaresborough, 1809) and (ii) William Gregory, *A Visible Display of Divine Providence; or, The Journal of a Captured Missionary* . . . (London, 2nd ed., 1801). See also George Pendle, 'The Lady Shore and the Duff', *History Today*, February 1955.

to defend her own possessions, and opened their eyes to the posibilities of profitable trade with Great Britain.[4]

For a number of years members of the British Government had considered assisting the inhabitants of Spain's South American Empire to overthrow their Spanish rulers. Finally, in 1806, Commodore Sir Home Popham and General Beresford, on their own initiative and without obtaining approval from London, sailed from Cape Town for the Plata and, on 27 June, captured Buenos Aires. Two months later the *criollo* population—not wishing to exchange Spanish for British rule—rose up and forced the invaders to surrender. Meanwhile, British reinforcements were on their way. The first contingent to arrive was too weak to attempt the recapture of Buenos Aires, so the officer in charge decided to disembark in the Banda Oriental. He attacked and took the small coastal town of Maldonado, which has a sheltered bay. Here the British ships anchored, and while awaiting further reinforcements the officers spent a pleasant time fishing and shooting. *Criollo* horsemen helped them to obtain food by lassoing cattle, of which they kept a considerable number grazing on the grassy headland where the fashionable seaside resort of Punta del Este now stands.[5]

At last, in January 1807, more troops reached Maldonado from England, under the command of Sir Samuel Auchmuty. But the combined British forces were still insufficient for the task of crossing the Río de la Plata and recapturing Buenos Aires. So Auchmuty moved against the smaller Spanish garrison of Montevideo instead. His artillery blasted a breach in the city walls, and his infantry attacked, on the night of 2–3 February. In the meantime the defenders had filled the breach with a huge pile of hides, laid one upon another, and many

---

[4] 'The life of the *criollo* population [of Montevideo] was obscure and almost claustral, with the result that the early history of Uruguay is exclusively Spanish, with none but Spanish performers on the stage—until the capture of Buenos Aires by British troops' (Eduardo Acevedo, *Manual de la historia uruguaya: Artigas*, 3rd ed. (Montevideo, 1942, p. 11). For an account of the Argentine aspect of the *invasiones inglesas*, see Pendle, *Argentina* (London, R.I.I.A., 1955), pp. 16–21.
[5] For the experiences of the British while waiting at Maldonado, see *Samuel Walters, Lieutenant R.N.: His Memoirs*, ed. by C. Northcote Parkinson (Liverpool University Press, 1949), pp. 51–52.

British soldiers lost their lives when storming it. Spanish casualties were even heavier.[6]

The British were in occupation of Montevideo from 3 February to 9 September 1807, during which time a host of British merchantmen lay in the harbour, for the report of the capture of the rich Spanish market of Buenos Aires by Popham and Beresford in 1806 had led speculators to dispatch large cargoes of merchandise to the Plata. The merchant ships had sailed from Great Britain before the news of Beresford's surrender and internment was received in London, and it was not until their arrival in South America that they learned that they could not now approach Buenos Aires, but must anchor on the much less prosperous Urguayan side of the river. 'Down at one fell swoop tumbled all the castles in the air,' wrote a Scotsman who had embarked on this 'export drive'. Stranded in Montevideo (which 'soon had more the appearance of an English colony than of a Spanish settlement') were

about six thousand English subjects, of whom four thousand were military, two thousand merchants, traders, adventurers; and a dubious crew which could scarcely pass muster, even under the latter designation. Hundreds of British ships were lying in the harbour. Buenos Ayres was still in possession of the Spaniards; but confident hopes were entertained that, when it should be heard at home that Montevideo was taken, a force would be sent out sufficient for the capture of the capital of so magnificent a country.[7]

In May and June 1807 General Whitelocke and the additional troops arrived; but in July their attempt to seize Buenos Aires failed ignominiously, and the British commander was compelled to agree to a complete evacuation of the Plata area, including the Banda Oriental.

Although the occupation of Montevideo by the British was so brief, it put new ideas into the minds of the population. Sir

[6] A young British sailor wrote a vivid description of the gruesome battlefield. See George Watson, *A Narrative of the Adventures of a Greenwich Pensioner* (Newcastle, 1827), pp. 32–36. For a detailed account of the campaign in the Banda Oriental see J. W. Fortescue, *History of the British Army*, vol. v (London, Macmillan, 1910), pp. 376 and 380–7.

[7] J. and W. P. Parish Robertson, *Letters on Paraguay* (London, 1838), i. 96–102.

Samuel Auchmuty's direction of affairs was enlightened and benevolent. He allowed the civil institutions to continue unchanged, and he took stern measures against any of his troops who maltreated the local citizens. A printing-press had been brought from England, and, under Auchmuty's patronage, this was used to print a weekly newspaper which appeared, with alternate columns of English and Spanish, under the dual title of *The Southern Star, La Estrella del Sur*.[8] The journal contained judicious propaganda in the form of articles critical of Napoleon (who was soon to invade the Banda's Spanish motherland) and others which drew a contrast between Britain's democratic methods of government and Spain's arbitrary rule. In the advertisement columns British merchants offered for sale the goods which they had intended for Buenos Aires but which now perforce were landed at Montevideo from the anchored ships: brandy and port, furniture and cloth, saddles and silk stockings, an enormous variety of manufactured articles. To assist trade, Auchmuty reduced the Customs tariffs. Never had Montevideo known such prosperity and activity.[9] British troops and merchants who crowded the formerly so isolated town made many friends. The Scotsman John Parish Robertson attended evening parties in the more well-to-do homes—'music, dancing, coffee-drinking, card-playing, laughter, and conversation'.[10] Captain Pococke fell in love with the young widow with whom he was billeted: 'her eyes sparkling, black as jet; her teeth equal and white. She wore her own hair, when dressed, as is the fashion of the country, in plaits down her back.'[11] 'Then they were so kind in their endeavours to correct the little blunders in Spanish of foreigners, without laughing at them, that they taught by example, at once good feeling and good manners.'[12] Many people in Montevideo regretted the enforced departure of the

[8] For a complete set of this newspaper, in facsimile, see Ariosto D. González, ed., *The Southern Star: La Estrella del Sur* (Montevideo, Instituto Histórico y Geográfico del Uruguay, 1942).
[9] For conditions in Montevideo during the occupation, see Carlos Roberts, *Las Invasiones inglesas del Río de la Plata* (Buenos Aires, Peuser, 1938), pp. 233–43.
[10] Robertson, *Letters on Paraguay*, i. 105.
[11] [Captain Pococke], *Journal of a Soldier of the 71st, or Glasgow Regiment . . .*, 2nd ed. (Edinburgh, 1819), p. 31.
[12] Robertson, *Letters on Paraguay*, i. 105–6.

invaders, after Whitelock's defeat; many British soldiers refused to obey the Commander-in-Chief's orders to embark for home, preferring to remain in this favoured region; and many businessmen, after the general evacuation to Britain, soon returned to the Río de la Plata to make their fortunes.

As for the Orientales: for them, life would never be the same again.

Chapter IV

THE STRUGGLE FOR INDEPENDENCE

SPANISH prestige in the Río de la Plata was further under-mined in 1808 by the news that Napoleon had installed a Bonaparte on the throne of Spain. The first effects were felt, however, not in Montevideo but on the other side of the river, in Buenos Aires, where the Spanish viceroy was deposed on 25 May 1810. The Spanish governor in the Banda Oriental repudiated that action. Montevideo was now the only remaining Spanish stronghold in the Plata area, and many years of warfare and confusion lay ahead.

When, in 1811, war began between the Spaniards at Monte-video and the independent junta at Buenos Aires, the people of the interior of the Banda Oriental fought side by side with the Buenos Aires forces against the Spaniards. Later the Orientales fought, time after time, against *criollo* invaders from Buenos Aires, who wished to annex their territory as an Argen-tine province, and against Portuguese or Brazilian invaders from southern Brazil. Throughout most of the century, too, the Orientales fought among themselves, and in the course of these internal struggles the Governments of Buenos Aires on the one hand and Brazil on the other frequently assisted one or other of the Banda's rival factions, which were sometimes more concerned to defeat their local opponents than to ex-clude foreign influence from the country. It is something of a miracle, indeed, that Uruguay should have emerged as an in-dependent republic at all. It is remarkable, moreover, that in the midst of the long succession of invasions and civil wars the Orientales did develop a distinctive national character of their own, and that suddenly at the beginning of the twentieth cen-tury this land of violence and chaos was transformed into a peaceful, orderly, democratic, and progressive republic, South America's first 'Welfare State'.

It was during the years of turbulence that the political foun-dations of modern Uruguay were laid. Early—as will be shown in the following paragraphs—the intransigence of the junta at Buenos Aires caused resentment and hastened the emergence of national sentiments among the Orientales, most of whom would otherwise have been quite content that their country should be linked with Buenos Aires in some form of federal system. Furthermore, the constant struggle between Buenos Aires and Brazil for possession of the Banda revealed—to many people in the Plata and the outside world alike[1]—the need for a buffer state to separate those two increasingly powerful rivals. Finally, it was during this period that the two political parties which today still dominate Uruguay's political life were born.

It will be impossible in this study to describe and explain all the ramifications of Uruguay's complex nineteenth-century history: only such events as had an important effect on the national evolution will receive attention.

The first of those major events, of course, was the outbreak of hostilities in 1811 between the loyal Spanish garrison at Montevideo and the independent junta at Buenos Aires. No sooner did the fighting begin than the whole of the interior of the Banda was up in arms against the Spaniards, who thus were confined within the town of Montevideo. In that emergency the Orientales discovered that they had a national figurehead: José Gervasio Artigas, a hawk-nosed, fair-skinned gaucho chieftain who, with a following of horsemen, had already made a name for himself by frequently raiding the southern border regions of Brazil. Artigas offered his services to the Buenos Aires junta, with whose forces he and his crowd of courageous, ill-equipped guerrillas agreed to collaborate in the siege of Montevideo. But the relations between the junta and the Orientales soon deteriorated. The junta looked upon themselves as the heirs of the old Spanish Vice-Royalty of the Río de la Plata (of which the Banda had formed a part), while Artigas (with the unofficial but acknowledged title of General) had no intention of accepting their dictates. The situation was

---

[1] For the first British efforts to prevent either Buenos Aires or Brazil from annexing the Banda Oriental, see J. Street, 'Lord Strangford and the Río de la Plata, 1808–1815', *Hispanic American Historical Review*, November 1953.

further complicated at this time by two new developments: Buenos Aires became preoccupied with a difficult campaign against the Spaniards in far-away Upper Peru, and the junta was alarmed by the news that the hard-pressed Spanish governor of Montevideo had appealed to the Portuguese in Brazil to come to his rescue. The junta therefore decided to seek an armistice with the governor. The armistice was concluded, and the Buenos Aires forces withdrew from the Banda; but the Portuguese invasion was under way, and it continued. This occasion, when the Orientales were abandoned by their allies to the mercy of the Spanish governor and the Portuguese, was the moment when they first felt that they really had a national destiny. General Artigas at once proved his genius. Collecting together thousands of his people, he led them from the neighbourhood of Montevideo in a wholesale exodus over the plains and hills; and thousands more joined the cavalcade as it travelled across the full breadth of the country. At the end of two months' journey, this extraordinary procession of gaucho horsemen, cartloads of women and children, Indians from the former Jesuit missions, pack-mules, and herds of cattle eventually reached and crossed the Río Uruguay into what is now the Argentine province of Entre Ríos. There the Orientales dwelt for some fourteen months in a makeshift encampment, with trees and the planks of their primitive ox-carts as their only shelter, living on beef and water.

But the armistice between Buenos Aires and the governor of Montevideo broke down, and in 1813 the siege of the latter town was resumed, with Artigas's renewed collaboration. Then, the Orientales having been invited to take part in an Assembly at Buenos Aires, Artigas dispatched five deputies, with instructions that they should secure autonomy for the Banda. The rejection of this demand brought the series of disputes to a head, and in January 1814, in the dead of night, Artigas struck his hide tents and again rode with his entire force away over the hills, leaving the Buenos Aires army to continue the siege as best they might.

So, for the second time, Artigas retired to the Río Uruguay, setting up his encampment on this occasion on the Uruguayan side of the river. From his camp he manipulated the affairs not

only of the Banda (excluding the urban district of Montevideo), but also of all of the up-river Argentine provinces,
which likewise had refused to accept the rule of Buenos Aires.
And even when in June 1814 the forces of Buenos Aires at last
forced Montevideo to capitulate (thereby removing the only
remaining vestige of Spanish power in the Plata area) and
were in turn expelled from the town by the Orientales, Artigas
did not go there from his distant headquarters. He was essentially a man of the open spaces, having no desire to live in
towns, an opponent of centralization (whether it were to be
enforced by others or by himself), a believer in the loosest form
of federal government that has ever been attempted. He was
content with the title of 'Protector of Free Peoples' that had
now been conferred upon him. John Parish Robertson who,
while travelling upstream to Paraguay, had been robbed by
the Protector's very irregular troops and therefore visited him
at his camp to claim compensation, wrote a description of the
scene:

I sailed across the River Plate, and up the beautiful Uruguay,
till I came to the Protector's headquarters of the so-called town of
the Purification. And there (I pray you do not turn sceptic on my
hands), what do you think I saw? Why, the most excellent Protector of half of the New World, seated on a bullock's skull, at a fire
kindled on the mud floor of his hut, eating beef off a spit, and drinking gin [i.e. *caña*, or rum, made from sugar-cane] out of a cow-
horn! He was surrounded by a dozen officers in weather-beaten
attire, in similar positions, and similarly occupied with their chief.
All were smoking, all gabbling. The Protector was dictating to two
secretaries, who occupied, at one deal table, the only two dilapi-
dated rush-bottom chairs in the hovel. . . . To complete the singular
incongruity of the scene, the floor of the one apartment of the mud
hut (to be sure it was a pretty large one), in which the general, his
staff, and secretaries were assembled, was strewn with pompous
envelopes from all the provinces (some of them distant 1500 miles
from that centre of operations), addressed to 'HIS EXCELLENCY THE
PROTECTOR'. At the door stood the reeking horses of couriers arriving every half-hour, and the fresh ones of those departing as often.
Soldiers, aides-de-camp, scouts, came galloping in from all quarters. All was referred to 'HIS EXCELLENCY THE PROTECTOR'; and his
excellency the Protector, seated on his bullock's skull, smoking,

eating, drinking, dictating, talking, despatched in succession the
various matters brought under his notice, with that calm, or de-
liberate, but unintermitted nonchalance, which brought most
practically home to me the truth of the axiom, 'Stop a little, that we
may get on the faster'.

Parish Robertson noted that Artigas was something more than
a rough gaucho: '[he] received me, not only with cordiality,
but with what surprised me more, comparatively gentleman-
like manners, and really good breeding'.[2]

Artigas graciously took Parish Robertson the round of the
hide huts and mud hovels of his encampment, and when the
Scotsman submitted his claim for compensation, the Protector
was as friendly as ever:

'You see', said the general, with great candour and nonchalance, 'how we live here; and it is as much as we can do, in these
hard times, to compass beef, aguardiente, and cigars. To pay you
6000 dollars [the amount of Robertson's claim] just now is as much
beyond my power as it would be to pay you 60,000, or 600,000.
Look here', said he; and, so saying, he lifted up the lid of an old
military chest, and pointed to a canvas bag at the bottom of it—
'There', he continued, 'is my whole stock of cash; it amounts to 300
dollars; and where the next supply is to come from, I am as little
aware as you are.'[3]

Artigas, by the strength of his personality, held his gaucho
federation together for a while; but, as it was against his principles to set up a powerful central authority, he was unable to
consolidate his widespread realm and consequently could not
repel the renewed invasion which began from Brazil in 1816.
For some three years he fought the better-equipped and better-
trained invaders; and he even declared war against his other
traditional enemies, the rulers of Buenos Aires. By the latter
move he lost the allegiance of several of his Argentine lieuten-
ants, so that finally, in 1820, he was obliged to seek asylum in
Paraguay where, a venerated figure, he died thirty years later.[4]
Before his exile, however, Artigas had stimulated in his native

[2] Robertson, *Letters on Paraguay*, iii. 101–3.   [3] Ibid. pp. 108–9.
[4] Regarding Artigas's long exile in Paraguay, see Carlos Pastore, 'Artigas
en el Paraguay', in Instituto Histórico y Geográfico del Uruguay, *Artigas:
Homenaje en el centenario de su muerte* (Montevideo, 1952).

land a sense of nationality that was destined to survive all the ravages and disasters that were still in store.

After the fall of Artigas, the Banda Oriental was officially annexed by Brazil and given the name of 'Cisplatine Province'. The alien Government ruled tolerantly, and European visitors to Montevideo in the early 1820's do not seem to have been surprised to find this Spanish colonial town under the domination of a Portuguese-speaking nation. Great Britain, it is true, never approved of the occupation of the Banda by the Portuguese and Brazilians; but other and more pressing matters nearer home had claimed the attention of the Foreign Office during the time of the latest invasion and annexation. Sir Charles Webster has remarked:

> For five years, therefore, Brazil was left in possession of the Banda Oriental. Buenos Aires was absorbed in the creation of the Argentine State. The instability of its Governments made effective action impossible. It was not until the independence of Argentina had been recognized by Britain and her growing trade had given Buenos Aires the wealth to buy ships and hire sailors, that the struggle for the Banda began again.[5]

During the intervening years there had been much scheming among Oriental exiles who wished to liberate their native land from the Brazilians; and at last, in April 1825, thirty-three patriots, the 'Immortal Thirty-three', crossed the river from Buenos Aires under the leadership of Juan Antonio Lavalleja. They at once received the support of the population of the Banda, and they progressed rapidly over the country towards the capital. The Buenos Aires authorities, informed of the patriots' success, sent warships and troops to assist them—it being understood that the Banda Oriental, when liberated from Brazil, would become one of the provinces of the Plata, under the hegemony of Buenos Aires.

For a long while the British Foreign Office had foreseen that war between Buenos Aires and Brazil over the Banda Oriental was again probable, and that the outbreak of hostilities would disrupt the whole of Britain's valuable commerce with the

---

[5] C. K. Webster, *Britain and the Independence of Latin America* (London, Oxford University Press, 1938), i. 69.

Plata ports. Their fears were now realized. In retaliation for
assistance to the Oriental patriots from Buenos Aires, the Brazilian fleet set up a blockade of the Río de la Plata which
effectively destroyed British trade in that area. The Foreign
Office therefore exerted their utmost influence in Rio de
Janeiro and Buenos Aires to obtain a peaceful settlement. As
early as February 1826 George Canning had suggested to
Lord Ponsonby (who was passing through Rio de Janiero on
his way to take up his post as Minister at Buenos Aires) that
'the town and territory of Monte Video should become and remain independent of either country, in a position somewhat
similar to that of the Hanseatic towns in Europe';[6] and it was
largely as a result of British mediation—and of Ponsonby's
'relentless zeal [in pursuing an] objective which he thought
important to his country'[7]—that in 1828 a treaty was finally
signed between Brazil and Buenos Aires whereby the new, independent República Oriental del Uruguay—a buffer state
with about 60,000 inhabitants—came into being.[8]

Nevertheless, the happy outcome of Britain's mediation
marked neither the beginning of peace in Uruguay nor the end
of foreign interference. An impression of the chronic disorder
that followed the official creation of the republic is conveyed
by Simon G. Hanson in these words:

> Of the twenty-five governments that guided the Uruguayan ship
> of state from 1830 to 1903, nine were forced out of power, two were
> liquidated by assassination and one by grave injury, ten resisted
> successfully one or more revolutions, and [only] three were free of
> serious disturbance during their periods in office.[9]

No sooner was the republic created than its creators began to
quarrel among themselves. Fighting broke out on a particularly large scale in 1836, when an insurrection against the
second President, General Oribe, was instigated by his prede-
cessor, General Rivera. The President had the help of Buenos
Aires; but France, which was at that time in the midst of a dis-

[6] Ibid. p. 138.   [7] Ibid. p. 70.

[8] For a convenient summary of British policy towards the Banda Oriental
see ibid. pp. 66–71. An Uruguayan account is provided by Luis Alberto de
Herrera, *La Misión Ponsonby* (Montevideo, 1930).

[9] *Utopia in Uruguay* (New York, Oxford University Press, 1938), p. 3.

pute with the Buenos Aires dictator, Rosas, gave its support to the insurgent movement. In 1838 Rivera made a triumphant entry into Montevideo and became President of the republic for the second time. Oribe escaped to Buenos Aires and then, as an officer in the service of Rosas, led an army against Rivera. Montevideo—named by Alexandre Dumas 'the new Troy'[10]—was besieged for nine years by forces from Buenos Aires. The French and Italian communities in the town raised legions of their own and fought strenuously in its defence, and Britain and France blockaded the Argentine ports. But it was only in 1851, when the Argentine general Urquiza revolted against Rosas, that the siege of the Uruguayan capital was lifted.

During these long years of warfare the rival groups wore distinguishing colours. Rivera's men adopted red, and the Colorados of present-day Uruguayan politics are their heirs.[11] Oribe's supporters wore white, and were the ancestors of the modern Blanco Party. The principles of the two parties have never been clearly defined, but traditionally the Blancos are supposed to have the approval of the conservative, rural, and clerical members of the population, while the Colorados profess to represent liberalism and progress. In general (though not invariably) Brazil aided the Colorados during the 1850's and 1860's, and Urquiza's army, which finally defeated Rosas at Monte Caseros in 1852, included 3,000 Brazilians as well as 2,000 Uruguayans.

The overthrow of Rosas freed the war-worn Oriental republic from Argentine invaders, but still did not bring lasting peace, or an end to foreign intervention. During the next sixteen years General Flores twice called upon the Brazilians to help him to power, and in return for their support he committed his country to join Brazil and Argentina in the war of 1865–70 against Paraguay. The Colorados now settled down to office more or less permanently, while the Blancos con-

[10] Alexandre Dumas, *Montevideo, ou une nouvelle Troie* (Paris, 1850).
[11] It was while fighting in defence of Montevideo that Garibaldi and his Legion first wore the red shirts which they subsequently made famous in Italy. For Garibaldi's life in South America, see G. M. Trevelyan, *Garibaldi's Defence of the Roman Republic*, Chapter II, and Newton Freitas, *Garibaldi en América* (Buenos Aires, Editorial Nova, 1946).

stantly revolted against them. In 1868 Flores and his principal opponent, a Blanco ex-President, were both assassinated. By 1880 the political situation had become so confused that Colonel Latorre resigned the presidency, declaring (it is said) that the Uruguayans were ungovernable.

In the wars and revolutions the number of combatants was never very large, and foreign travellers were able to obtain permission to pass through the rival lines. When, in December 1845, the Argentine educator Domingo Faustino Sarmiento visited the beleaguered Montevideo, he compared conditions in that town favourably with the 'barbarie' then prevailing in his own country. There were foreigners of many nationalities in Montevideo: liberal *émigrés* from Argentina, English businessmen, English, French, and German artisans, Basque labourers. For Sarmiento, the cosmopolitan composition of the population, the commercial activity and free trade signified civilization and progress.[12]

[12] A. W. Bunkley, *The Life of Sarmiento* (Princeton University Press, 1952), pp. 239–40.

Chapter V

THE BIRTH OF THE WELFARE STATE

In spite of Sarmiento's favourable impression, the country's economy developed very slowly until the end of the nineteenth century. Travellers from Europe, however, were not entirely dissatisfied with the appearance of Montevideo. There were three good hotels—though Captain Richard Burton would not lodge at the best of them, the 'Oriental', because 'during the cholera days it made the mistake of refusing to admit the wife of the British Minister, although a surgeon of the United States squadron certified that she was not attacked by the epidemic'. The shops in the central streets—'mostly French, and full of glitter and attractions'—were up to European standards.[1] Drainage was defective, but there was a supply of wholesome water, and gasworks were built. In Burton's day a single tram-line led to the bull-ring: a few years later other lines extended to the residential suburbs,[2] so that by 1892 nearly 4,000 horses and mules were at work on the lines.[3] Railway construction was started but made slow progress until 1875, because British investors lacked confidence in the stability of the country. Electric lighting was then installed. Small local industries—manufacturing such articles as footwear, matches, and beer—were established and received tariff protection.

The interior of the republic was almost totally neglected. The production of wool was lucrative, but estancieros made little attempt to improve their estates. Only an insignificant area of the land was cultivated. There were no roads outside the towns, and no bridges. Rivers had to be crossed on horseback.

You enter the river. . . . As the stream deepens, you at last kneel upon the saddle. The horse may have to swim only in the middle

---

[1] Richard F. Burton, *Letters from the Battle-fields of Paraguay* (London, Tinsley, 1870), pp. 105–6 and 118.
[2] Robert Crawford, *Across the Pampas and the Andes* (London, Longmans, 1884), p. 19. Crawford was in Uruguay in 1871.
[3] Mulhall, *Handbook of the River Plate*, p. 610.

part of the river, though in floods it will be often from one bank to another. In which case you sit down on the horse with the water to your chest, and you must on no account check the horse, but leave the bridle loose, as the result would be immediately to drown him, for nothing drowns so quickly as a horse. . . . If the distance across is too great, and you find it too much for him, you must slip off behind him, hold on by his tail, keeping well back, and he will be certain, thus relieved of your weight, to draw you to land. . . . The passage of these rivers, in woody places, is sometimes 'enlivened' by deserters popping at you as you cross, especially in war time; such places being convenient spots for robbing travellers.[4]

If the river had been rendered too dangerous by recent rains, the horseman would dismount on the bank and wait for the flood to subside.

Uruguay remained backward, too, in social development. Elections to Congress were controlled by the ruling faction; no legislation existed for the protection of labour; and only about one child in fifty attended school. Shocked by this state of affairs, however, in the second half of the century a number of enlightened young men began to prepare the way for more civilized conditions. Prominent among them was José Pedro Varela, who in 1867 visited the United States, where he met the educational pioneer Horace Mann and became the disciple of Sarmiento (at that time Argentine Minister in Washington). No sooner had he returned to Montevideo than Varela was addressing meetings and writing articles, demanding the introduction of universal free education on the United States model. He argued that until primary education was properly organized, Uruguay could not evolve into an orderly democracy. Surprisingly, his ideas attracted the attention of the dictator, Colonel Latorre, who in 1877 issued a decree whereby the whole Varela plan became law. Varela was appointed inspector of public instruction, with full powers to carry out his programme. The reforms had been opposed by doctors of the university, who had a vested interest in the old order, and, because of their liberal and secular character, by the Catholic Church. Indeed, in the opinion of one well-

---

[4] J. H. Murray, *Travels in Uruguay* (London, Longmans, 1871), pp. 64–65. The author was in Uruguay in 1868.

known Uruguayan writer, the opposition was so powerful that Varela's proposals might never have been passed by a democratic Congress.[5] Thus, on one occasion at least, military dictatorship operated in the service of democracy. Varela remarked:

> Tyranny is not the creation of Latorre: it is the natural result of my country's social state. The surest way to fight dictatorship, is by transforming intellectual and moral conditions, and this can only be done in the schools. And as . . . the people will not entrust me with the direction of education, I must receive it from whomever will do so, no matter who he may be. I shall not destroy today's dictatorship, . . . but I shall prevent dictatorships in the future.[6]

In his official post Varela worked tirelessly to organize the new primary school system. Never a robust man, he exhausted his strength and died—an acknowledged national hero—in 1879, aged thirty-four.

Meanwhile, another young reformer was rising to ever greater prominence. This was José Batlle y Ordóñez. Born in 1856, Batlle became a political journalist. In 1886 he founded his own newspaper, *El Día*, in whose columns he diagnosed his country's ills and proposed remedies for them. He became the leader of the Colorado Party, and was twice elected President of the republic. One of his disciples defined Batlle's policy as the adoption of 'all that is reasonable, human and practical in the Socialist programme'.[7] For several decades Batlle was 'the human centre around whom everything moved and was resolved'. In appearance a massive figure, with a thoughtful head, he was essentially a man of action.

Endowed with real political talent, his outstanding characteristic nevertheless was an athlete's energy. He dominated not so much by the vastness of his conceptions as by executive forcefulness, admitting no obstacles. Having been accustomed for many years to daily agitation in the streets and in the press, when he entered the government he still continued to be a fighter, for whom official power was a means, not an end [and the presidency was] a valu-

---

[5] Alberto Zum Felde, *Proceso Intellectual del Uruguay* (Montevideo, Editorial Claridad, 1941), p. 134.

[6] Ibid. p. 136. For a detailed study of the 'Valerian System' see Zum Felde's *Evolución Histórica del Uruguay*, 3rd ed. (Montevideo, 1945), pp. 253–64.

[7] Zum Felde, *Evolución Histórica*, p. 232.

able instrument for putting his ideas into practice, not merely a neutral and representative position.[8]

This interpretation is confirmed by a description of Batlle in action shortly after he became President for the second time:

> The present writer well remembers hearing him, on the first day of the great general strike of 1911, addressing the strikers from the balcony of Government House at Montevideo.
>
> He told them that were it not for his high office he would be among them and with them; counselled them to stand firmly for their rights; and wound up by warning that any acts of intimidation or violence on their part would not only injure their just cause, but expose the guilty parties to extremely severe punishment.
>
> By way of underlining this last wholesome admonition, Martial Law was immediately declared.[9]

One of the crucial events in Batlle's long campaign to convert chaotic Uruguay into an orderly and progressive democracy occurred during his first period as President (1903–7), when, in 1904, he effectively crushed a Blanco revolution by force of arms. That victory was decisive, and thereafter Batlle's position within his party and in the nation was secure. On the expiry of his term he was therefore able to make an unprecedented announcement, which was in keeping with his principles: unlike his predecessors, he stated that he would observe the clause in the still valid but habitually ignored Constitution of 1830 which prohibited a President from succeeding himself in office.[10] He then sailed for Europe and remained there for the next four years studying the Swiss and other methods of government. When he returned to Uruguay to become President for the second time (1911–15), the ideas which he had been developing experimentally in *El Día* since 1886 were mature. Many people were now in agreement with them and were ready for the beginning of a new era. Without delay, Batlle recommended that the state should have a monopoly of

---

[8] Ibid. p. 227.

[9] Gordon Ross, *Argentina and Uruguay* (London, Methuen, 1917), p. 71.

[10] For the principal features of the Constitution of 1830 see Eduardo J. Couture, *La Constitution uruguayenne de 1952* (Paris, Extrait des Cahiers de Législation et de Bibliographie Juridique de l'Amérique Latine, nos. 11–12), pp. 9–15.

insurance, electric light and power. He demanded an eight-hour working day, a compulsory whole day's rest for every five working days, regulations to control conditions of work, several important educational reforms, and the reorganiza-tion of the state bank. He introduced legislation to permit divorce at the will of the wife and to abolish capital punish-ment and bull-fighting. He advocated the creation of a state mortgage bank, the construction of state railways to supple-ment the British-owned lines, and a state monopoly in the manufacture of alcohol and tobacco. He proposed that insti-tutes and experimental stations should be established to assist the basic industries, and that increased protection should be provided for domestic industry. He recommended old-age pensions, workmen's compensation, indemnification for dis-charged employees, and legislation to protect illegitimate children. These innovations, together with Batlle's anti-clerical policy, outraged the conservatives, some of whom went so far as to suggest that the President was insane. 'But no one, even those who feared most from his persistent political and financial adventures, has ever even so much as hinted that his policy was dictated by other than honestly intentioned conviction.'[11] An indication of the extent to which the national temper had changed was that, after 1904, there was 'not a sign of overt rebellion in a situation over which only a few years ago the whole country would have been engaged in a fratri-cidal struggle'.[12]

Among Batlle's many public expressions of opinion, the fol-lowing, quoted from the press of the time, are typical: 'There is great injustice', he declared, 'in the enormous gap between the rich and the poor.' 'Our population may be divided into those who have received more than they deserve and those who have received less. . . . But this does not mean that a man is either exploited or an exploiter. The inequality is not de-liberate on the part of the more fortunate.' 'The real source of inequality is in the difficulty of arriving at a just distribution.' 'The gap must be narrowed—and it is the duty of the state to attempt that task.'[13] Batlle disapproved of foreign ownership

---

[11] Ross, *Argentina and Uruguay*, pp. 33–34.   [12] Ibid. p. 70.
[13] Hanson, *Utopia in Uruguay*, p. 22.

of public services and industry, and was confident in the ability of the state to replace the foreign capitalist.

None of Batlle's social reforms could have been effective in practice, however, if he had not reformed the methods of government. He argued that the Colorados must make themselves worthy of popular support by behaving democratically and he was convinced that the country could never be a real democracy until it was provided with a new Constitution. He believed that the ills of nineteenth-century Uruguay were largely due to corrupt elections and excessive presidential power. By securing reasonably honest elections, he removed one of the motives for revolution. He next proposed to eliminate the office of President.

Chapter VI

THE EVOLUTION OF THE
WELFARE STATE

THE CONSTITUTION

SINCE 1911 constitutional reform has been the principal issue in Uruguayan politics. This subject must therefore receive more attention in the present study than would be necessary in a book about almost any other country.

Convinced that presidential power led to dictatorship and revolution, José Batlle y Ordóñez had decided that the Presidency should be abolished and replaced by an Executive Council, on the Swiss pattern. A number of young Colorados —influenced by Batlle's personality rather than by his arguments—supported their leader's plan, while others were unable to accept it, so the party split into two factions on this fundamental question. The Blancos ridiculed the suggestion that Uruguay should be governed by a committee. Consequently it was evident that—for the time being, at least— Batlle would have to accept a compromise, and at a constituent convention in 1917 agreement was reached that executive power should be divided between a President and a National Council of Administration. The President was to be elected by direct popular vote[1] for a term of four years, and would not be eligible for immediate re-election The nine members of the Council were also to be elected by the people. They were to serve for six-year terms, one-third of the membership being renewed every two years. At every biennial election the party receiving the largest number of votes was to be granted two seats on the Council while the third seat was to go to the leading minority party. By this arrangement it was ensured that the Blancos, even if they did not receive one-third of the total votes, would always be represented and therefore be deprived of an excuse for armed insurrection. Under this Constitution,

[1] Under the Constitution of 1830, the President was elected by Congress.

which was officially promulgated in January 1918 and became effective in 1919, the President was placed in charge of the Ministries of the Interior, Foreign Relations, and National Defence, while the Council was given control of finance, education, health, public works, and industry. Thus the concentration of executive power in the hands of one person or group of persons was prevented; but the 'elaborate machinery for eliminating personal influence involved the paradox that only a strong and determined man could make it work'.[2] The 1918 Constitution provided considerable autonomy for the departments or provinces and municipalities. It also separated Church and State.

Batlle died in 1929, but his personality continued to exert a powerful influence, and even today he seems to be present at every election.[3]

At the time of the economic depression of the early 1930's the Colorados were still in power, and in 1933 the President, Gabriel Terra, formed the opinion that the Constitution was preventing him from undertaking the economic and other measures which the circumstances demanded. Government deficits had increased alarmingly; unemployment was growing; the autonomous state institutions devoted to real estate loans, public health, and pensions were approaching bankruptcy; and meat exports had fallen in volume and value. Moreover—as the original critics of the Constitution had foretold—the National Council of Administration was constantly disorganized by internal squabbles between its Colorado and Blanco members and made little or no attempt to co-ordinate its actions with those of the other branches of government. Therefore in March 1933 Terra carried out a coup d'état, dissolved the Council and the legislature (i.e. the General Assembly),[4] and governed by decree. This event was a shock to many Uruguayans, who had been proud of their country's

[2] F. A. Kirkpatrick, *Latin America: a Brief History* (Cambridge University Press, 1938), p. 160.

[3] Russell H. Fitzgibbon, *Uruguay: Portrait of a Democracy* (New Brunswick, N.J., Rutgers University Press, 1954), p. 122.

[4] For the present composition and functions of the General Assembly see below, pp. 40–41.

democratic record during the previous twenty-nine years.

A new Constitution was now drawn up and was adopted after a plebiscite in 1934. Under this Constitution the National Council of Administration was abolished, its main powers being transferred to the President. But Terra was obliged to reward the important Blanco faction that had supported his coup d'état, and so, to enable them to have a share in the government, the revised Constitution provided that the President must select three of the nine members of his Cabinet from the leading minority party, and that one-half of the seats in the Senate must be given to that party. Thus the Blancos in the Senate were in a position to prevent any effective action by the President if they so wished, and it was evident that this clause would have to be amended at some future date. Terra allowed himself to be unconstitutionally re-elected in 1934. He continued to govern by decree until the expiry of his second term in 1938, when he was succeeded by his brother-in-law, General Alfredo Baldomir. Meanwhile the economic situation had improved; but during 1933-8 economic recovery was not confined to Uruguay, and it is doubtful whether Terra was responsible for the improvement.[5]

Under President Baldomir the Blancos took every opportunity to obstruct legislation. They violently criticized the Colorado policy of collaborating with the United States in hemisphere defence, and protested when, in January 1942, the Government severed relations with the Axis Powers. To counteract the threat of disorder, Baldomir, in defiance of the Constitution, postponed the elections which should have been held in February 1942, replaced the three Blanco members of the Cabinet with his own supporters, and dismissed the General Assembly. He also decided that yet another new Constitution should be prepared. Baldomir permitted the holding of elections in November 1942, and the constitutional amendments were submitted to the electorate on that occasion. The main purpose of the reform was to prevent the opposition minority from obstructing government action. With this in

[5] For an interesting account of the Terra régime see Philip B. Taylor, 'The Uruguayan Coup d'État of 1933', *Hispanic American Historical Review*, August 1952, pp. 301-20.

view, the opposition's right to occupy automatically half the seats in the Senate was cancelled. At the November elections a Colorado, as usual, won the Presidency, and the revised version of the Constitution was approved. Uruguay now returned to the democratic way of life which Terra's action had interrupted.

The influence of José Batlle y Ordóñez was apparent throughout the text of the Constitution as it stood in 1942. After an opening passage wherein the nature of the state was described, there was a summary of the individual and social guarantees to be enjoyed by the Uruguayan people. The chief items in this section are as follows:

(1) The death penalty does not exist in Uruguay.

(2) Prisons are places for re-education rather than for punishment.

(3) The spoken and the written word are inviolable. (Abuses, however, will be punished according to law.)

(4) Arbitrary arrest, searches, and seizures are forbidden.

(5) Freedom of movement in all parts of the nation is assured (subject to the law).

(6) Equality of treatment is assured to all religions.

(7) Children are to be protected from physical, intellectual, or moral neglect, and their exploitation is prohibited.

(8) Parents have the same obligation towards their natural children as towards those born in wedlock.

(9) It is the duty of all citizens to take care of their health and to help others in case of illness.

(10) The state will assist those whose finances will not permit adequate medical attention.

(11) Labour will receive the special protection of the state, and 'Every inhabitant of the republic, without prejudice to his liberty, has the duty of applying his physical or mental energy in such manner as to redound to the general welfare'.

(12) The organization of trade unions will be assisted by law.

(13) Social security laws will assure to all workers adequate financial protection in cases of accident, illness, or forced unemployment.

(14) Primary education is free and compulsory.

(15) In the event of foreign attack or civil commotion, the President of the Republic may, for the safety of the nation, order anyone's arrest and removal from one part of the country to another; but he may not impose punishment. Any action that the President may take under this emergency power must be reported to the General Assembly within twenty-four hours.

(16) The Constitution may be amended only after the proposed amendments have been submitted to and approved by the electorate.

Constitutional reform became a live issue again in July 1951, when the principal Colorado faction, the Batllistas, and the chief Blanco faction, the Herreristas, signed a pact whereby they agreed to recommend the establishment of a plural executive—known in Uruguay as *el Colegiado*. The reason for this *volte-face* by the Herreristas—who had always ridiculed the idea of the *Colegiado*—was that, after yet another Colorado victory in the elections of 1950, they realized that the Blancos' only chance of sharing in the government of the country, from which they had been excluded for so long, would be by replacing the (Colorado) President of the republic by some form of council of government wherein the Blancos, as the leading opposition party, would be entitled to a certain number of seats. The Batllistas accepted the assistance of the Herreristas in carrying out this reform for two reasons: first, because the Colorado majority in the newly elected General Assembly was insufficient to ensure effective one-party rule and, second, because the support of the Herreristas would enable them to fulfil one of the fundamental requirements of the original Batllista creed.

The text of the new Constitution[6] was submitted to a plebiscite in December 1951 and was approved, though by a relatively small majority.[7] The Constitution came into force in March 1952. The principal innovations were as follows:

---

[6] See A. J. Peaslee, ed., *Constitutions of Nations*, 2nd ed., vol. iii.

[7] For an examination of the plebiscite results see Couture, *La Constitution uruguayenne de 1952*, pp. 33–36.

1. The presidency of the republic ceased to exist. Instead, the executive was to consist of a National Council of Government of nine members, six of whom would come from the political group which received the greatest number of votes at the elections, and the other three from the second largest party. The Council was to be elected every four years by direct popular vote.

2. Members of the majority party in the National Council were to take it in turn to occupy the presidency of that body for a period of one year. The President of the Council would preside over its meetings and sign official documents together with the Minister or Ministers concerned. Otherwise, the President's powers would not differ from those of the other members of the Council, none of whom would be entitled to issue orders of any kind.

3. The National Council was to nominate the Cabinet, which would consist of nine Members of State. (At the time of the promulgation of the new Constitution, the Ministers were: Interior, Foreign Relations, National Defence, Public Instruction and Social Welfare, Industry and Labour, Livestock and Agriculture, Public Works, Public Health, and Finance.)

4. The post of *intendente* (or chief executive) ceased to exist in the nineteen Departments (or provinces) of the republic. In future the Departments were to be administered by departmental councils, whose membership would be regulated on the same majority and minority party principle as that governing the composition of the National Council. The election of departmental councils would take place every four years, coinciding with that of the National Council.

5. The National Council was to be responsible for the nomination of the directors of the state-owned banks, industries, and public services on the majority and minority party principle. These appointments were to be submitted to the Senate for comment, and, when approved, would be valid for four years.

6. The General Assembly would appoint a Tribunal (*Tribunal de lo Contencioso-Administrativo*) to watch over the national Government and the boards of directors of the state-owned enterprises. The Tribunal would have power to annul any illegal acts by those bodies.

7. The national and departmental governments would not be entitled to approve budgets, enter into new commitments, authorize increases in salaries, &c. during the twelve months preceding elections.

Thus the 1952 Constitution introduced the two-party system of the *Colegiado* not only into the national executive, but also into provincial government and the administration of the state-owned financial and industrial enterprises and public services. As all those appointments terminate simultaneously every four years, and as the date of their termination coincides with the expiry of the mandate of the General Assembly, 'il y a donc lieu tous les quatre ans un renouvellement de toutes les couches supérieures du gouvernement et de l'administration publique'.[8]

It will be apparent that the new Constitution established a number of safeguards (in addition to those already existing) against the abuse of power by men in authority. Whether, in practice, the additional precautions have favoured or discouraged efficiency in the management of the country's affairs is a question which can be, and often has been, debated. Certainly one result of the constitutional reform has been a slowing down in governmental processes. For example, when a Minister and his staff have drawn up a project for legislation, the dossier is submitted to a technical two-party committee of the National Council for consideration. If the committee approve, the project will then be discussed by the Council in plenary session before being passed to the General Assembly. Or it may be returned to the Minister for revision, or it may be rejected. Rejection does not create a political crisis. This method of initiating legislation has been criticized on the ground that the deliberations of the two-party committee and Council cause delay. But as the meetings of the Council are fully reported in the daily press, the procedure does at least provide an opportunity for public opinion to influence the Executive's decisions.

Apart from the important modifications mentioned above, the principal features of Uruguay's earlier Constitution (1942)

[8] Ibid. p. 39.

have remained almost unchanged—except, of course, that the National Council now fulfils the duties that formerly were the responsibility of the President.

The Electorate. Every citizen, male or female, is entitled to vote on reaching the age of 18. This right is also accorded to foreigners who have obtained their legal citizenship, or who have resided in the country for 15 years. Legal citizenship is granted after 3 years' residence to those who are married and who reside in the country with their families and after 5 years' residence to those who are unmarried.

The Legislature. The General Assembly consists of a Chamber of Representatives and a Senate. The duties of the General Assembly include that of approving, modifying, or rejecting the Budget presented by the Executive.

The Chamber of Representatives has 99 members. They are elected by a system of proportional representation, but by Departments, each of the 19 Departments having at least 2 members. Deputies serve for 4 years, and are eligible for immediate re-election. The minimum age for deputies is 25. The Chamber has the exclusive right of arraigning members of the National Council and the Cabinet before the Senate, and, in the event of a vote of no confidence, the resignation of the accused is required.

The Senate has 31 members elected by a system of proportional representation. Senators serve for four years, and are eligible for immediate re-election. They must be at least 30 years of age.

Legislation may be proposed by the National Council (through a Minister) or by any member of either House of the General Assembly. Only the Executive, however, may initiate legislation increasing the number of public servants or their remuneration. Other Bills which involve extra-budgetary expenditure must indicate how the corresponding revenue is to be found.

Bills which have been approved by the General Assembly are passed to the National Council for promulgation.

The General Assembly elects a Permanent Committee which meets during the Assembly's recess. The Committee's duty is to warn the National Council and the Cabinet if they should be guilty of violating the Constitution or the laws. If the situation should be considered serious, the Committee may call for a special session of the Assembly.

The National Council also may summon the General Assembly to special session.

Justice. There are no juries in Uruguay. All judges must retire at the age of seventy.

The Supreme Court of Justice has 5 members, who are chosen by the General Assembly. The members must be at least 40 years of age, and lawyers with 10 years' practice, or 8 years' service on the bench. The judges of the Supreme Court serve for 10 years and are ineligible for re-election until 5 years after the expiration of their term. The Supreme Court deals with all cases of offence against the Constitution, and those arising on the high seas or involving the principles of international law; civil actions brought by foreign diplomats; and cases which reach the Court on appeal. It exercises general supervision over the entire judicial system, and is entitled to declare laws unconstitutional.

The Supreme Court appoints Courts of Appeal (which have 3 members), Civil Judges, and Justices of the Peace.

SOCIAL LEGISLATION

Batlle y Ordóñez maintained that the employer should always set the public welfare above private gain; that the employer should pass on a greater share of his profit than formerly to his employees; and that the employer and the state should aid the poor, the sick, the old, and the young. As a result of Batlle's preaching in his newspaper, *El Día*, and his long domination, in and out of office, of national politics, the trade unions at a comparatively early date gained from employers many improvements in conditions of labour, so that in the second and third decades of the twentieth century Uruguay already had to its credit an imposing body of enlightened legislation. When the legislators set to work, they were often too ambitious, and too confident in the efficacy of mere legislation; but Batlle had persuaded them that Uruguay, although a small republic, was destined to take a place in the vanguard of social progress. Some of the laws enacted under the influence of this remark-

D

able man are summarized below.[9] In practice, they have not always operated as effectively as their creators would have wished; and some of them have imposed what appears to be an excessive charge on the national economy. Nevertheless, these laws—with a number of modifications and additions—continue to be in force today and, together with the Constitution, they form the foundation of the Uruguayan 'Welfare State'.

Hours of work. On 17 November 1915 the 8-hour working day and the 48-hour working week were instituted. Subsequent laws have reduced those working hours in certain trades.

Hours of rest. On 19 November 1920 a minimum of one day's rest in every week was granted to all drivers of motor-cars and carriages, and to all domestic servants. On 10 December 1920 it was made compulsory that all classes of workers should have 24 hours of rest after every 6 days' work. On 22 October 1931 commercial employees became entitled to the *semana inglesa*, or 'English week'—i.e. a holiday on Saturday afternoons, in addition to the day's rest on Sunday.

Holidays with pay. On 27 April 1933 a law was promulgated granting annual holidays of a fortnight with pay to 'white-collar' workers. This was the first of a long series of laws on the subject. On 13 June 1941 the right to holidays with pay was extended to seamen and various classes of urban manual workers. Holidays with pay are now general.

Minimum wages. On 18 November 1926 a minimum wage was established for workers in the ports. There followed similar legislation for other industries. On 12 November 1943 the minimum wage was officially defined as one 'which is considered necessary in relation to the prevailing economic conditions in a given place, to ensure an adequate standard of living to the worker, so as to satisfy his physical, intellectual, and moral needs'. In that same month, procedure was instituted for the creation and operation of Wage Boards to fix minimum wages and settle wage disputes in the various in-

[9] The information in this section is based on Alberto Sanguinette Freire, *Legislación social del Uruguay*, 2nd ed. (Montevideo, 1949). For a complete and detailed record of social legislation now in operation, see Eduardo J. Couture and others, *Legislación vigente en el Uruguay*.

dustries, the members of the Boards being nominated by the state, the employers, and the employees. Once a wage is so determined, it automatically becomes law. Criticism is often expressed that the Boards 'have in recent years tended to award unjustifiably large wage increases, thus raising Uruguay's already high costs of production, lowering her ability to compete in international markets, and contributing to the inflationary spiral'.[10] Furthermore:

Through the years, as the government has designedly expanded its industrial and commercial enterprises, it has come increasingly to face a dilemma with regard to organized labor: the government's consistent attitude has been pro-labor, but it has itself become more and more an employer of labor; the two attitudes have at times come into basic conflict.[11]

In the fixing of minimum wages there is no co-ordination between the various industries and trades. Anomalies therefore occur.

Family allowance. In November 1943 provision was made for the payment of a 'family allowance' to 'employees, workmen, or labourers' for each of their children (whether legitimate or illegitimate)[12] up to the age of fourteen, or up to the age of sixteen in the case of a child still studying at school or at a technical college. Family allowances were to be administered by special Compensation Funds, which were to derive their income from a levy on employers' pay-rolls.

Compensation on dismissal. By a law of 6 June 1944 commercial employees obtained the right to one month's salary for each year's service, with a maximum compensation of six months' salary. Subsequent legislation established similar compensation for employees in all other urban occupations. On 16 October 1946 it was decreed that 'the dismissal, without just cause, of a rural workman of good character, will give him the right to indemnification'. The indemnity was fixed at half a month's salary per year's service for the first three years' service, and one month's salary for every year's service in excess of three years.

[10] G.B., Commercial Relations and Exports Dept., *Uruguay*, p. 72.
[11] Fitzgibbon, *Uruguay*, p. 95.
[12] It has been estimated that 27 per cent. of births are illegitimate.

Workers' accident compensation. By a law of 21 July 1914 employers were required to take adequate measures to protect their employees while at work, and later legislation stipulated the technical precautions applicable in a large number of industries. On 28 February 1941 it was proclaimed that 'every employer is responsible in civil law for accidents met with by his employees as a result of their work or while at work'. Government Departments, Municipalities, and Public Corporations were required to insure their staff in the State Insurance Bank. Private employers were not compelled to insure, but were called upon to prove their financial capacity to meet their obligations under the law.

Unemployment compensation. On 17 May 1939 a law was passed establishing the right of shipwrecked seamen to receive compensation, and many laws were drawn up subsequently to regulate the distribution of work at the docks, in the public services, &c., with the purpose of minimizing the risk of unemployment. On 12 December 1944 an Unemployment Compensation Fund was created for the meat-packing industry. The members of the Council controlling the Fund were to be nominated by the Government, the employers, and the workers. The Fund was to be financed by means of duties levied on the industry's exports and by a $9\frac{1}{2}$ per cent. levy on wages, $7\frac{1}{2}$ per cent. being payable by the employers and 2 per cent. by the workers. On 10 December 1945 a similar Fund was created for workers in the wool and hide warehouses.

Old-age pensions. A law introducing old-age pensions was passed on 11 February 1919. Pensions were to be paid by the state to 'every person who has reached the age of sixty and to anyone [of no matter what age] who is totally incapacitated and in poverty'. Funds for this pension scheme were to be obtained by the taxing of employers and the owners of large landed estates, and by taxes on playing-cards and spirits.

The most ardent Batllistas would like to see still further welfare legislation. For example, they have demanded that a healthy and adequate diet for rural workers be defined and made compulsory; that employees in the state-owned corporations should receive a share in the profits of those enterprises; that school teachers be paid a special bonus in proportion to the number of pupils at their schools; and that heads of families be granted a small monthly allowance towards the expenses of each of their children attending school. It is argued that these and other similar reforms would be in the spirit of Batlle's teaching.

PUBLIC HEALTH

At the present time Uruguay—a particularly healthy land, unafflicted by tropical diseases—has no national system of health insurance; but Batlle believed that the nation was responsible for the care of the sick, and—partly as a result of his teaching—the medical services are now well developed. The Faculty of Medicine at the University of Montevideo is large, and has a high reputation. The huge Hospital de Clínicas, though for many years its equipment was incomplete, has long been a landmark, rising above the trees of Montevideo's Batlle Park; and there are numerous smaller hospitals providing more beds per thousand of the population than are available in other Latin American countries. In Uruguay, as in several of the other republics, a United States mission has collaborated with the local authorities to improve the health services in working-class districts of the capital and in the provinces.

STATE OWNERSHIP

Batlle y Ordóñez was convinced not only that the state was capable of operating public services and industrial and commercial enterprises, but also that state ownership was in the public interest. This conviction became a feature of the Colorado 'ideology', and today the state operates a large number of so-called 'autonomous entities' (*entes autónomos*), or public corporations. For example, the state controls electricity and telephones. It refines petroleum and manufactures alcohol and cement. It directs a meat-packing plant and the processing of fish. It controls the railways, the principal banking institutions, and insurance.[13] The United States Tariff Commission, in a report on Uruguayan economic conditions, commented:

[13] The *entes autónomos* are dealt with individually in the chapters on Industry, Transport, and Finance.

Public monopolies have been employed in other South American countries principally as fiscal agencies and as sources of governmental income. In Uruguay, however, the motives appear to have been different; the system of State enterprises was inaugurated to procure certain economic and social benefits for the Uruguayan people, such as low-cost insurance, wider employment, low interest rates, and a sanitary and inexpensive meat supply for the city of Montevideo. These agencies have been used also to limit the control of foreign capital over the industrial life of the nation and to assure a degree of independence from foreign sources of supplies.[14]

Some of the state enterprises have continually operated at a loss, being maintained largely by government subsidies. Others, however, have shown a profit, and the net income from state-owned undertakings between 1937 and 1940 averaged more than 10 million pesos annually. Indeed, a frequent criticism is that several of these concerns (the State Insurance Bank and the Electricity Authority in particular) have been so preoccupied with the making of profits that they have neglected their obligation to expand and cheapen their services.

The *entes autónomos*—each with its own board of directors and its own budget—have been relatively free from political interference. The Constitution of 1952 decreed that the National Council of Government should nominate the boards, selecting the members from the two leading political parties on the majority and minority principle.

A problem has arisen from the great size of the civil service. It was recognized that to maintain efficiency among such a very large number of state employees, some special machinery was necessary. Therefore in 1943 a Statute of Functionaries was devised, providing for the appointment (by the head of the state) of a Directorate, whose functions would be to formulate general policy and to act as a court of appeal. Furthermore, in each Ministry and each state-owned corporation there was to be a junta composed of high officials, serving as an advisory body. And each Ministry and corporation was to have its own tribunal to supervise the recruitment of staff,

---

[14] U.S. Tariff Commission, *Economic Controls and Commercial Policy in Uruguay* (Washington, 1945), p. 11.

promotions, and conditions of employment. In practice, these many safeguards seem to have imparted excessive rigidity to certain aspects of employment; but honesty and diligence are considered to be greater in the civil service in Uruguay than in most of the other Latin American countries.

The Constitution recognizes that trade unions have the right to strike.[15] Civil servants (including employees of the *entes autónomos*) are not entitled to form trade unions, or to strike—but, in practice, they do strike.

[15] Concerning trade unions, see below, p. 89.

Chapter VII

LIVESTOCK, AGRICULTURE, AND
FOREIGN TRADE

THE influx of foreign capital into Uruguay is not large, and so the country depends almost entirely on its pastoral and agricultural exports for foreign currency. The comparatively high standard of living enjoyed (at least, by the inhabitants of the Montevideo region) is therefore closely related to the export trade; and this state of well-being always seems vulnerable, because pastoral and agricultural produce is subject to sudden fluctuations in world demands and prices. To reduce the nation's dependence on external trade, successive Governments have encouraged the development of domestic industry —by means of protective tariffs, import controls, exemption from import duties on machinery, and preferential rates of exchange. But as there are no local sources of petroleum or coal, and no heavy industry, Uruguay is still obliged to import virtually all of its fuel, industrial raw materials, and machinery; and these essential supplies have to be paid for with the produce of the ranches and farms, helped by foreign currency brought by tourists.

LIVESTOCK

When Hernando Arias shipped cattle and horses to the deserted pastures of the Banda Oriental in 1603, he showed that he recognized that the wealth of South America did not consist solely in precious metals, and he has been described by the Uruguayan author Zum Felde as the first of the colonials to possess a really American outlook. The herds multiplied to such an extent that it is estimated that at the time of the founding of Montevideo in 1726 there were about 25 million head of cattle in the Banda. The manner of life of the people, when colonization began, was determined by the presence of these huge herds which roamed over the countryside. The men lived on horseback. They had merely to throw their lasso or their *boleadoras* to secure the meat and leather which were almost their only requirements. Riding over land which was still unfenced and whose ownership was still undefined, they developed 'unsocial' characteristics. In 1806 when John Mawe, an enterprising British merchant and mineralogist, was interned on an estancia 160 miles distant from Montevideo, the cattlemen were still almost nomads. Mawe wrote:

Ten thousand head [of cattle] are allotted to four or five Peons... Breeding is alone attended to; neither butter nor cheese is made, and milk is scarcely known as an article of food. The constant diet of the people, morning, noon, and night is beef, eaten almost always without bread, and frequently without salt.[1]

Mawe stated that the doors of the peons' 'wretched dwellings' often consisted of 'a green hide stretched on sticks', and he added:

The furniture of these poor hovels consists of a few skulls of horses . . . and of a stretched hide to lie upon. . . . Fuel in some parts is so extremely scarce that the following strange expedient is resorted to for a supply. As the mares in this country are kept solely for breeding, and are never trained to labour, they generally exceed, in a great degree, the due proportion; a flock of them is frequently killed, and their carcases soon becoming dry, are used as firing (with the exception of the hides and tails which, when properly prepared, are packed for exportation).[2]

In spite of wire fencing, the disappearance of the nomadic gaucho, and the colonization of virtually the entire territory of the republic, certain features of life in the Banda Oriental as described by John Mawe at the beginning of the nineteenth century still persist. For instance, the consumption of meat per inhabitant is about 290 lb. a year—the highest in the world. The production of milk, butter, and cheese is still inadequate, though dairy-farming has greatly increased. In 1947 a British Agricultural Mission to South America reported that, although there were many small dairy farmers in the neighbourhood of Montevideo (with Friesian cattle, of Dutch, North American, or Argentine origin), in other parts of the republic

[1] *Travels in the Gold and Diamond Districts of Brazil*, pp. 26–27.
[2] Ibid. pp. 27 and 28.

milk was merely produced as a by-product of beef. At that time the Government deliberately favoured dairy-farming; but later, because of the decline in the supplies of meat for export,[3] they tried to encourage the breeding of beef cattle by such measures as the subsidizing of freights for the transport of animals from the more distant parts of the republic, the granting of assistance in the preparation of winter pastures, and the fixing of attractive prices. Beef cattle are mainly Herefords.

Two factors were chiefly responsible for the decline in the size of beef cattle herds in the 1950's:[4] first, high world prices for wool stimulated sheep-breeding,[5] and, second, the government policy of subsidizing the production of wheat caused much grazing land to be transferred to agriculture.[6] An increase in the domestic consumption of meat further reduced the surplus available for export. Stock-breeders continued to be disheartened by the difficulties encountered in delivering their cattle to the stockyards and by the inadequacy of research and technical services.[7]

Production of wool has risen about 75 per cent. during the last twenty years,[8] and economists have pointed to the danger that an excessive concentration on the breeding of sheep for wool would bring about a serious economic crisis if world prices were suddenly to fall. Nevertheless, prices were well maintained after the Second World War and during and after the Korean War, and wool is still the greatest source of national income.

In addition to raw wool, Uruguay is now a leading exporter of wool tops.[9] As this was a new industry, it received government assistance until 1959 in the form of a preferential ex-

[3] For comparative export figures, see Appendix III.

[4] It is estimated that while there were about 8·3 million head of cattle in Uruguay in 1951, there were only about 7·42 million in 1956.

[5] The number of sheep increased from about 18 million before the Second World War to about 23·3 million in 1956.

[6] For comparative figures of livestock and wheat production, see Appendix I.

[7] U.N., ECLA, *Economic Survey of Latin America, 1955* (New York, 1956), p. 55 and G.B., Commercial Relations and Exports Dept., *Uruguay*, p. 55.

[8] Production of wool reached about 200 million lb. (greasy basis) in the mid 1950's (Commonwealth Economic Committee, *Wool Intelligence*, September 1956, p. 477).

[9] Exports of wool tops rose from 2·4 thousand tons in 1950 to 15·9 thousand tons in 1956.

change rate, which provoked frequent protests from other textile manufacturing countries. From 1953 to 1959 the United States imposed an 'anti-dumping' duty on Uruguayan tops.

After studying Uruguay's sheep-breeding industry the British Agricultural Mission of 1947 reported:

The emphasis in sheep farming is on the production of wool and consequently Merino, Corriedale and Polworth and other crosses predominate. Hampshire Down sheep are said to be declining in numbers: Romney Marsh, based on exportation from New Zealand, are still in favour and differ somewhat from the English type, being more on the leg and a finer bone. Purchases from England, however, are occasionally made to reintroduce size and strength of bone. Although limestone is more abundant in Southern Uruguay than in the Argentine, all imported livestock deteriorate in quality after the second generation, calling for continual introduction of fresh blood.[10]

The British Mission also remarked that the Uruguayans were still great lovers of horses, and that the peon on the estancia was supplied with six or seven horses for his daily work. 'Native ponies are reared in large numbers throughout the country.... Lightness and speed are essentials required. Work on the farms and in the towns is done by horses of Percheron type but, even with them, the lighter type (the Bordelais) is preferred.'[11]

AGRICULTURE

John Mawe, referring to the state of agriculture in 1806, wrote:

It is rare to meet with an inclosure, even for a kitchen garden, much more so for a cornfield. They generally choose their grounds for tillage by the banks of a rivulet, so as to have one side or sometimes two sides bounded by it; the remainder is fenced in the most clumsy and bungling manner imaginable. Ploughing is performed by the help of two oxen yoked to a crooked piece of wood, about four inches in diameter, and sown, without any previous attempt to clear it from noxious seeds. . . . Indian corn, beans, melons, etc.

---

[10] G.B., Ministry of Agriculture and Fisheries, *Report of the South American Agricultural Mission*, p. 31.
[11] Ibid.

are all treated in a similar way. The wheat, when ripe, is cut down with sickles, and gathered into heads of sheaves . . . and a herd of about twenty mares is driven in, which, being untamed, are easily frightened and made to gallop round. At this pace they are kept by means of whips for four or five hours, until the corn is trodden out of the ears. . . . In this state it is left until it blows a brisk gale; and then the winnowing is performed by emptying baskets of the mixed grain and chaff at an elevation of eight feet from the ground. While the chaff is borne away by the current of air, the grain falls, and at the close of the operation, is sewed up in green hides.[12]

Agriculture developed late in Uruguay. Throughout the nineteenth century the turbulent state of the country delayed the growth of rural communities. Moreover the soil in general is not so rich as that of the Argentine provinces on the other side of the river, and it is therefore more suited to cattle and sheep-raising than to farming. Local traditions still are pastoral rather than agricultural. Even in the big towns a garden lawn is referred to not as a *césped*, which is the correct Spanish term, but as *pasto*, or pasture.

After the Second World War, the Government's guarantee of remunerative prices for cereal crops caused an increase in output, and for several years Uruguay has grown more wheat than is required for local consumption.[13] An adverse effect of this official policy of agricultural subsidization has been referred to above, in regard to cattle-raising. Furthermore, the wheat subsidies (subsequently lowered) became an excessively heavy item of national expenditure, and, because of high production costs in Uruguay, the exportable surplus of wheat could only be disposed of with difficulty, large losses being incurred when world prices fell.

Other cereal crops are maize, sunflower seed, flax (linseed), oats, barley, and rice.

Fruit-growing is extensive, the principal fruits being peaches, oranges, apples, pears, and grapes.

The chief farming districts are in the south, in the Departments of Soriano, Colonia, San José, and Canelones.

[12] Mawe, *Travels*, pp. 32–33.
[13] In recent years wheat production averaged more than 800,000 metric tons. Local consumption amounts to only about 400,000 tons. (Information received from Banco de la República and U.S. Department of Agriculture.)

Not only did agriculture in Uruguay begin late, but technical progress has been slow. The Inter-American Economic and Social Council has stated that 'in order that the manufacturing industries may permanently draw manpower from agriculture, it is essential that those still employed in the production of foodstuffs and raw materials increase not only their per-capita productivity but also the total absolute output of their sector.'[14] The growth of urban industry in Uruguay now needs to be counterbalanced by improved methods of agriculture, and further mechanization—which was retarded by the interruption of importing during the Second World War and the subsequent shortage of dollars and sterling. The British Agricultural Mission of 1947 reported on local requirements:

The hills and undulating land are somewhat like England and the implements required are very similar. The heavy rainfall and undulating hilly land make half-tracks very necessary with interchangeable implements designed and built on the unit principle for a medium sized wheel tractor of between 20 and 30 h.p., the implements being designed to fit the tractor when working with either wheel or half-tracks. A tool bar for row crop work should usually be included with the set of implements, maize, beans and potatoes being row crops of great importance. Small tractors are also urgently required for cultivating between vines and fruit trees, where narrow cultivation for deep work is very important.[15]

The fundamental issue in Uruguayan life today is still, as it was in the time of Artigas, an unresolved struggle between the capital city and the interior of the country. One-third of the total population of the republic lives in Montevideo, and the capital continues to draw people away from the land. Recent Governments have been criticized for their neglect of the rural population. The following extract from the newspaper *La Mañana* is a typical expression of this point of view, though rather exaggerated:

The national economy cannot much longer survive the con-

---

[14] Inter-American Economic and Social Council, *Secretariat Report on Economic Conditions and Problems of Development in Latin America* (Washington, Pan American Union, 1950), p. 9.
[15] *Report of the South American Agricultural Mission*, pp. 31–32.

tinual deterioration from which rural life, in all its aspects, is suffering.

The gradual depopulation of the towns and villages of the interior; the lack of specialized workers and the alarming decline in the number of available labourers to attend to the cattle and for agriculture; the malnutrition, the high rate of infant mortality, the unhygienic living conditions; the great number of persons over fourteen years of age who are utterly uneducated, or who have barely had from one to three years' elementary education; the existence of a rural school wherein the system and methods of teaching are totally inadequate for local needs; the complete absence of medical and social welfare organizations in communities that number several thousand persons, who receive very few of the benefits of this kind that are dispensed in the capital; the high rate of illegitimacy which in no way corresponds with the state of social advancement which our legislation seems to indicate. . . . We possess laws and public organizations designed to protect the young; to colonize the interior; to encourage production; to spread education, public health, and preventive medicine; to raise, in short, the social and economic values of the entire republic. But the effect of these laws and the action of these organizations rarely cover the whole of the national territory. In very many cases, so far, legislation and government have been directed only to the people of Montevideo.[16]

FOREIGN TRADE

The degree of prosperity enjoyed by Uruguay, year by year, depends on the fluctuating world prices of her pastoral and agricultural products and variations in the terms of trade. Other external factors affect the balance of payments and the pattern of trade. Thus during the Second World War the United Kingdom purchased almost the whole of Uruguay's meat surplus; as a result of the concentration of British industry on war-time needs, imports from the United Kingdom were drastically reduced; and, consequently, at the end of hostilities Uruguay had an accumulated sterling balance of about £17 million. Meanwhile the war had virtually eliminated continental Europe both as a market and as a source of imports, and the United States had become for the first time the leading and generally the only buyer of Uruguayan wool.

[16] *La Mañana* (Montevideo), 18 August 1950.

After the war the United States continued to be the chief customer for wool, and the United Kingdom still took most of the meat, together with other products, such as hides and linseed. But in the immediate post-war years Uruguay's dollar reserves were quickly expended in urgent purchases from North America, and so the United Kingdom soon resumed its former position as the principal supplier of imported goods. After the outbreak of war in Korea, however, the pattern again altered. By the end of 1950 wool exports to the United States had once more produced a substantial dollar reserve (amounting to over $100 million), and therefore a renewed increase in imports from North America occurred. While the dollars from wool sales were flowing in, the effects of a shortage of sterling began to be felt. The shortage was caused by three principal factors. First, heavy imports—not only from the United Kingdom, but from various other countries—had been paid for in sterling; second, Uruguay had devoted a large part of the previous reserves to the purchasing of the local railways from their British owners; and third, after the breakdown in Anglo-Argentine negotiations on the price of meat in the middle of 1950, the Uruguayan Government had associated itself with Argentina and suspended meat shipments to the United Kingdom. Simultaneously, British trade with Uruguay was adversely affected by the revival of European—and particularly German—competition; by Uruguay's efforts to fulfil a number of bilateral agreements with several European countries, and with Japan and Brazil; and by the growing insistence of Uruguayan industrialists, such as the leaders of the woollen textile industry (which had expanded greatly during the Second World War), that the importing of many types of consumer goods should be severely curtailed. Import and export regulations multiplied and became more and more complex, until the whole system was abolished in 1959.[17]

The kinds of goods imported into Uruguay vary from year to year in relative importance. In general, imports of raw materials consist mainly of raw cotton and cotton yarns, burlap, iron and steel (ingots, sheets, and strip), artificial silk

[17] See below, Chapter XII.

yarns, newsprint, and chemicals. Since 1939 petroleum has replaced coal as the chief fuel. The principal building materials are timber and structural iron and steel. Foods and beverages include *yerba mate*, bananas, and sugar. Machinery and spares are major items.

The tourist trade has long been a source of foreign exchange. The state owns several hotels, and the Government takes pains to attract holidaymakers from abroad. In normal years about 120,000 foreigners visit Uruguay's beaches and hills. They come chiefly from Argentina (there are no beaches or hills in the vicinity of Buenos Aires), but also from southern Brazil (where the climate is less temperate) and, in smaller numbers, from land-locked Paraguay. An attempt is being made to encourage tourist traffic from the United States.

Montevideo itself is a popular resort, because although it is a large city, it is a pleasant and breezy place, and the riverside and seaside are within easy reach. From the centre straight boulevards, bordered by plane trees and acacias, go out to the suburbs and to the eucalyptus woods, the sand dunes, and the blue sea. In the suburbs the little houses are white, with brightly coloured shutters. The general effect is gay, and in summer at midday people in bathing costumes fill the open-air restaurants along the shore. The further beaches are so large that at week-ends people from Montevideo make use of them for horse-riding, motoring, and camping. They park their cars on the hard, smooth white sand. An awning is stretched from the side of each car, and in its shade the family eat and sleep. Big hotels are dotted along the coast as far as fashionable Punta del Este and, more sparsely, beyond.

Tourists from Argentina have several convenient means of travelling to and from the Uruguayan resorts. There are frequent air services between Buenos Aires and Montevideo; diesel trains and omnibuses connect the Uruguayan capital with the coast; and there is a daily air service to Punta del Este in summer. Every night river steamers cross the Plata between Buenos Aires and Montevideo. And there are daily boat services from Buenos Aires to the upstream Uruguayan port of Colonia, with a bus connexion between the latter town and

Montevideo along an excellent highway. Many Argentines take their motor cars to Uruguay, where they are granted special facilities for petrol, and many of them own holiday villas at Atlántida, Punta del Este, and other resorts. Tourists also go to the inland village of Colonia Suiza (near the river port of Colonia), a delightful settlement of Swiss origin, famous for its butter, cheese, and honey.

The tourist traffic from Argentina declined and was finally stopped altogether during the régime of President Perón (1946–55). At the beginning of that period Perón and his supporters urged that Argentines should take their holiday in their own country, and this propaganda was supported by the great improvement that had been effected in the highway system linking Buenos Aires with the distant Argentine beaches, southern lakes, and western mountain spas. The improved communications had encouraged the building of luxury hotels at the Argentine resorts. Perón then launched a campaign to try to prevent Argentine political exiles from being allowed to attack his régime on the Uruguayan radio and in the newspapers. (Uruguay has always been a favourite refuge for Argentine exiles.) Obstacles were placed in the way of people wishing to travel to Uruguay. In 1951 the Argentine Government required that all persons going there should possess passports. (Previously Argentine and Uruguayan citizens journeying between the two countries had only to show their local identity cards when embarking and disembarking.) Finally, as the Uruguayan Government refused to limit the freedom of speech of exiled anti-Peronistas, additional restrictions were imposed by Argentina which made travel virtually impossible. No sooner had Perón been overthrown, however, than all restrictions were removed, and Argentine visitors poured into Uruguay again. Thereafter the only hindrance to the tourist trade was the steady rise in prices in Uruguay. For some years the Government has tried to offset this disadvantage by granting a subsidy to hotel-keepers on foreign visitors' bills, the allowance being passed on to the guest as a special discount.

E

Chapter VIII

INDUSTRY AND TRANSPORT

INDUSTRY

THE degree to which Uruguay's prosperity is dependent on foreign trade has been indicated in the previous chapter. In Uruguay—as elsewhere in Latin America—the conception has long prevailed, that a nation which relies almost completely on the willingness and ability of foreign countries to take its meat, wool, and grain in exchange for manufactured articles has not yet emerged from the 'colonial' stage in its development. 'Progress' is more or less identified with 'industrialization'.

José Batlle y Ordóñez was the first Uruguayan to preach that his country should be rendered independent of foreign suppliers by means of industrialization. Local industry, he argued, should be encouraged by the Government, and it should be financed exclusively by Uruguayan capital. A rival school, however, has consistently maintained that the nation's real wealth will always be in its livestock and crops, and that the growth of urban industry, by diverting attention from these natural riches, will tend to impoverish the land. In a monumental book on this subject one of the most persuasive opponents of industrialization, Julio Martínez Lamas, exclaimed: 'The great sources of Uruguayan wealth are not to be found in the city, but in the fields. As far as the production of wealth is concerned, the potentialities of the city are almost negligible.'[1] He divided industry into two categories. The first category comprises the various kinds of 'food-processing' which, with the working of leather, were the original type of industry in Uruguay and are a 'legitimate' method of enhancing the value of the vital resources of the land before exporting them in exchange for foreign currency, gold, and essential imports. (The wool-combing industry now also serves this pur-

[1] Julio Martínez Lamas, *Riqueza y pobreza del Uruguay*, 2nd ed. (Montevideo, 1946), p. 41.

pose.) The second industrial category consists of the factories which manufacture for home consumption goods which otherwise would be imported. The development of this second type of industry was opposed by Martínez Lamas, who denied that the Uruguayans could augment their national wealth by aping foreign industrial states and reducing the importation of manufactured goods. He argued that the real vitality of Uruguay's pastoral and agricultural communities was being sapped by industrialized Montevideo. Nevertheless, the industrial expansion recommended by Batlle has continued.

As has already been stated,[2] Uruguay possesses no raw materials (except certain kinds of stone, used in building and in the manufacture of cement) apart from those which come from livestock and agriculture, and the country has no known deposits of coal or petroleum. The potential sources of hydroelectric power have not yet been fully exploited. Therefore the newer industries—which successive governments have protected and encouraged—remain to a very large extent dependent on imported raw materials and fuel. It is estimated, however, that in spite of these disadvantages at least 75 per cent. of manufactured goods now sold in Uruguay are produced in domestic factories. Reference is made to the more important industrial products in the course of the present chapter.

Electricity. It is apparent that if Uruguay is to attain 'economic independence' by means of industrialization, the first requirement is that it should increase its hydro-electric output.

The earliest electric-light plant was installed in Montevideo in 1886 and was the first electric plant to be set up in South America. Street lighting was soon introduced, and private houses were wired. In 1897 the Government acquired the electric-power industry, which until that time had been owned by private companies. Today a state-owned corporation named Administración General de las Usinas Eléctricas y los Teléfonos del Estado (or UTE) has a monopoly of all electric services. The law of 1912 which gave this monopoly to

[2] See above, pp. 5, 48.

UTE was sponsored by Batlle y Ordóñez. The principal object was not to obtain revenue for the state, but to provide (in Batlle's words) 'buena luz y barata aunque el Estado no gane; buena luz y barata aunque el Estado pierda!' (good and cheap light, even though the state may make a loss.) In practice, however, UTE made handsome profits year after year, and it was accused of neglecting to supply adequate facilities in the interior of the republic. This omission is now being remedied.

As the low, rolling countryside of Uruguay is not generally suited for hydro-electric development, most of the electric installations until quite recently have been dependent on imported coal or oil for the generation of power. Nevertheless, a large water-power site does exist in the centre of the republic, on the Río Negro, 150 miles to the north of Montevideo; and in 1937 work began on the construction of a dam at this spot. The dam, measuring 3,850 feet, was completed in 1945, and it created the largest artificial lake—87 miles by 18 miles—in South America. The Río Negro project was planned by the German firm of Siemens, and was carried out by that company until the beginning of the Second World War. A North American concern (Westinghouse) then undertook to complete it and to provide a transmission line from the power station of Rincón del Bonete to Montevideo. The installation is also designed to assist in flood control, irrigation, and river navigation.

In 1956 the International Bank for Reconstruction and Development made a loan to UTE which was partly to be used for the construction of a second electric plant on the Río Negro at Rincón de Baygorría, some 53 miles downstream from the Rincón del Bonete station. This new plant was to derive its power mainly from the Bonete reservoir and was intended to increase Uruguay's electric output by about one-quarter. To some extent the scheme answered the accusation that UTE neglected the interior of the republic, for the chief object of Baygorría was to supply electricity not to Montevideo but to the industries which in recent years have been opened up in provincial regions, where the consumption of power has risen by over 16 per cent. annually since 1947. These post-war provincial industries include a cement plant, a tannery, a sugar refinery, fertilizer plants, and paper factories.[3]

Another project which has been frequently discussed is an ambitious scheme for building a dam and an international bridge at the Salto Grande rapids on the Río Uruguay. It is proposed that the hydro-electric installation at Salto Grande should be financed equally by the Uruguayan and Argentine Governments and that the plant would supply electricity not only to the western area of Uruguay but to the neighbouring districts of Argentina.

UTE is also responsible for Uruguay's telephone services. The telephone was first tried in Montevideo in 1878. Private telephone companies began to be formed in 1882, and in the 1890's Montevideo had more telephones per capita than any other city in South America. In 1920 there were 24,000 subscribers in the whole country, served by 28 companies. By that time, however, the law had been passed which established that the services of posts, telegraphs, and telephones were to be exploited exclusively by the state, and the Government gradually took over the private enterprises. In 1949 UTE had about 65,000 subscribers, but there was a waiting list of more than 18,000; circuits in the interior of the republic were quite out of date; and cross-country connexions were deficient. These shortcomings were the result partly of the organization's conservative policy and partly of the difficulty experienced in importing new equipment during the war. In 1959 the U.S. Development Loan Fund granted a loan which was to be devoted to the improvement of UTE's telephone system.

Petroleum. A state-owned corporation, the Administración Nacional de Combustibles, Alcohol y Portland, known as ANCAP, imports a large volume of crude oil and has a monopoly of the refining of all oil brought into the country, which it undertakes at its refinery of La Teja, Montevideo. Thus ANCAP refines all the oil imported by the big foreign groups (Shell-Mex, Standard, &c.), but these companies are then allowed to market their motor oil under their own trade

[3] Bank of London & South America, *Fortnightly Review*, 24 November 1956, pp. 742–3.

names. Uruguay's oil requirements have been growing steadily in recent years under the combined influence of an increasing population, further mechanization of road transport and farming, and rising oil consumption by the railways.

Oil is imported chiefly from the Caribbean area and the Middle East, with smaller quantities from several South American countries. Uruguay began to purchase crude oil from Chile in 1950, the advantage being in the relatively short tanker voyage. Montevideo is only 3½ days' voyage from the Magellanes area where the Chilean cargo originates, compared with 13 days' steaming from Venezuela and 30 days' from the Persian Gulf.

ANCAP has a fleet of barges and tankers.

Gas is produced by an old-established British company at Montevideo. The coal for the gas-works, of course, is imported.

Cement. ANCAP is responsible for the manufacturing of cement. A factory for this purpose has been constructed in the Department of Lavalleja, near Minas, where suitable limestone is available. Uruguay has been self-sufficient in Portland cement since 1957.

The Meat industry. The food-processing industries are still the most important industrial group in the republic.

In the pre-refrigeration period, the principal product of the meat-processing industry was jerked beef—i.e. beef that had been salted and dried. In 1847, however, Baron Justus von Liebig invented a method of manufacturing meat extract, and in 1863 a German engineer named G. C. Giebert, who had previously lived in Uruguay, returned there to start producing the extract by Liebig's process. In 1864 he made his first exports. In 1865 a company was formed in London to exploit the process on a large scale at Fray Bentos, on the Río Uruguay. The business was profitable from the start, but the extract could not serve as a substitute for fresh meat, and *Chambers's Journal* on 19 January 1867 published the comment: 'The Extractum Carnis, which is something like treacle in consistency and glaze in flavour, is fit for nothing but soup; and we want something with more body in it for hard-working men and women.' In 1871 fat and hides were still the mainstay of the business at Fray Bentos; but in that year the factory produced over 6 million lb. of jerked beef and 571,000 lb. of Liebig's meat extract.

Refrigeration made it possible for Argentina[4] and Uruguay to develop their great modern meat-packing and meat-exporting industries. In Uruguay there are four large packing-plants—*frigoríficos*—which, together, account for 95 per cent. of the national output. One of these *frigoríficos*, situated at Fray Bentos, is British-owned; the other three are at Montevideo. One of the latter is owned by the state; the other two were created by North American interests. The *frigoríficos* prepare tinned meats, frozen and chilled meats, extracts of beef, guano, dried blood, fats, glue from the hooves, and many other by-products.

The state-owned plant, the Frigorífico Nacional, was established in 1928 with the purpose of reducing the dominance of the industry by the powerful foreign companies. It was intended that the Frigorífico Nacional—which was given a monopoly of slaughter for the supply of the capital—should assist the local producer by raising the price of livestock, while at the same time, and rather contradictorily, lowering the price of meat for the benefit of consumers in Montevideo. At the outset the concern was financed by a loan. Profits were to be divided as follows: 50 per cent. in shares to livestock sellers in proportion to the quantity sold to the Frigorífico Nacional; 25 per cent. for dividends on investment; and 25 per cent. for distribution among employees. The board of directors was to consist of five members nominated by the Government, the Municipality of Montevideo, and the Department of the Interior, and by two of the producers' organizations, the Asociación Rural and the Federación Rural.

In the 1950's the foreign-owned *frigoríficos*, which produced only for export, were closed or put on short-time working for long periods because of the shortage of animals (referred to in Chapter VII), inability to compete with the high prices offered to breeders by the Frigorífico Nacional, and wage disputes. The two U.S. companies closed down completely in 1957, and in the following year legislation was passed transferring their plants to a co-operative society of former employees.

[4] Cf. Pendle, *Argentina*, p. 47.

Fish-processing. The state's participation in the fishing industry, by means of state-owned trawlers and a factory which produces small quantities of tinned fish, fish meal, fish oil, &c., seems to have been one of the least successful of state enterprises. This organization (the Servicio Oceanográfico y de Pesca, known as SOYP) was created with the object of providing the population with abundant fish at cheap prices. SOYP has constantly operated at a loss, and little progress has been made in persuading the Uruguayans to modify their preference for meat.

SOYP now operates the sealing industry[5] on the Isla de Lobos. One of the largest colonies of sea-lions in the world is to be found on this island and on a smaller islet beyond it. It is accepted as being the only place in the world where the Common Sea-lion (*Otaria bironia* or *jubata*) and the Southern Fur-seal (*Arctocephalus australis*) live together. At the height of the breeding season the colony numbers between 100,000 and 200,000 animals. The males of the common sea-lion seen by Norman Pelham Wright when visiting the Isla de Lobos were of vast proportions, some of them measuring nine feet long or more. The very rare fur-seals are smaller, and are believed to eat not fish but crustacea, octopus and cuttlefish, algae and seaweeds. The two species mingle in perfect harmony on the island, but there is no interbreeding. Huge numbers of the animals are killed periodically for their valuable pelts and oil; but in spite of this they are not alarmed by the presence of man, and are easy to approach. Indeed, the Uruguayan Tourist Department now considers the colony a tourist attraction.

Montevideo is the anchorage during the winter months of various whaling flotillas owned by British and Scandinavian companies that operate in the South Atlantic.

The Dairy industry. In recent years the dairy industry, encouraged by the Government, has considerably expanded. A National Council of Dairy Farmers—the Cooperativa Nacional de Productores de Leche, or CONAPROLE—was created in 1935 by the expropriation of the private firms then existing. To finance the expropriation, CONAPROLE issued

[5] See above, p. 1.

debentures which were guaranteed by the state. The five directors of the organization are elected by the milk producers themselves.

CONAPROLE—which collects milk from the farmers for pasteurization, and delivers it as milk, butter, or cheese to its customers—has had difficulty in meeting the growing demand which results from an increasing population and a rising standard of living. The industry has been hampered by scarcity of skilled labour and by high labour costs. Dairy-farming is practised particularly in the neighbourhood of Montevideo and Colonia.

Other food-processing industries. There are many wheat flour mills, and also rice and maize mills. A large number of small establishments manufacture sufficient bread, biscuits, spaghetti, and vermicelli for local needs.

The cooking habits of the Uruguayan people create a demand for large quantities of vegetable oils. The Spanish War and the Second World War cut off supplies of imported olive oil, so the number of crushing-mills producing oils from sunflower seed, peanuts, &c. has greatly increased.

Raw sugar is imported, and local refiners have a special charter and receive special privileges from the Government. Sugar beets are grown, in inadequate quantities, in the Departments of Maldonado and Canelones.

Beverages of various kinds are produced by a large number of firms, and the industry is protected by high import duties. Wine is made from local grapes by many small establishments, and is sufficient for domestic requirements. Two large breweries likewise produce adequate supplies of beer for local needs, using, mostly, home-grown barley. The largest manufacturer of spirits is ANCAP, who make *caña* and brandy. There are several small establishments producing whisky and gin, but these drinks are normally imported from Great Britain, and brandy from France.

Textiles. Formerly, because of the large-scale rearing of sheep in Uruguay, the textile industry was almost entirely woollen and worsted. The principal woollen textile firm, Campomar y Soulas, established their first mill (La Nacional) about ninety years ago. The activities of this firm have now extended to Argentina. Wool-combing for export has been referred to above.[6] The wool used in the combing and spinning industries, and in the weaving of cloth and blankets, is domestic; the machinery is imported.

The revival of international competition since the end of the Second World War has shown that Uruguay's woollen and worsted industry is somewhat over-developed, and therefore considerable opposition to the importation of woollen and worsted textiles has arisen.

The two largest cotton mills—Primera Hilandería del Uruguay (owned by Campomar y Soulas) and a mill that is affiliated to the Argentine Alpargatas Company—together with a quantity of small establishments produce one-third or more of local requirements in cotton textiles. Local production, however, consists chiefly of the heavier types of cotton textiles. Nearly all the finer types, for clothing, are imported.

Raw cotton is imported chiefly from the United States, and also from Paraguay.

Rayon and other synthetic fibres are increasingly used, though the finest qualities are lacking.

Almost the entire textile industry—which is the most important urban industry in the republic—is situated in Montevideo.

Tyres. One of Uruguay's largest and most profitable private enterprises is the Fábrica Uruguaya de Neumáticos (FUNSA) which manufactures sufficient rubber tyres, tubes, and mechanical rubber goods to satisfy the domestic market. FUNSA was established in the late 1930's, with the technical direction of the United States Goodrich Company. The local company was granted a nine-year monopoly and is protected by very high tariffs.

Chemicals. To a considerable extent the local chemical industry is devoted to elaborating imported chemicals for consumer use. The biggest local supplier of chemical products is the Instituto de Química Industrial, a state-owned organization situated in Montevideo. The Instituto was created in 1912 to engage in research; but when the First World War interrupted chemical imports, there was a demand for domestic

[6] See above, pp. 50–51.

production. As a result of a decree of 1915 a small factory for commercial purposes was authorized, and practical training of students began. Production of fertilizers started in 1922, and by 1924 locally made sulphuric acid was available in relatively large quantities. Today local products include alcohol, sulphate, chloride and carbonate of soda, chloroform, collodions, sulphuric ether and acid, superphosphate, commercial sulphate of iron, benzol, toluol, and naphthalene, nitric acid, hydrochloric acid, caustic soda, and ammonia.

By 1938 Uruguay was self-sufficient in the production of such basic chemicals as sulphuric acid, hydrochloric acid, and alcohol, and in the production of superphosphates, casein, soap, glycerine, and matches. Furthermore, Uruguay manufactures cattle dip, disinfectants, insecticides, candles, cleaning and polishing materials, varnishes, cosmetics, and paint. Local linseed oil is used exclusively in the five local paint factories. The Montevideo Gas and Dry Dock Company produces certain coal-tar crudes as by-products. The Instituto Nacional de Higiene (a non-profit-making government agency) makes biological preparations.

Wood and paper. The wooded areas of the republic amount only to about $1\frac{1}{2}$ million acres, and over 70 per cent. of Uruguay's wood requirements has to be imported. Local production of lumber is concentrated along the waterways. There is a milling centre in the vicinity of Montevideo, and a small plywood industry. Reafforestation is encouraged by the Government.

There are many small furniture and carpentry shops. The Fábrica Nacional de Papel and several other mills produce printing paper, wrapping paper, paper board, containers, stationery, &c. Newsprint is imported.

Leather. In this land of cattle and horses, the old gauchos used leather so extensively that Zum Felde has referred to the gaucho period as 'The Age of Leather'. At the founding of Montevideo, houses were constructed with leather. Moistened leather was used instead of nails, rope, and wire, which were unheard of. Doors and beds were of leather. And the horsemen used leather sacks and wineskins. General Auchmuty, in his official dispatch reporting the capture of Montevideo by the British troops in 1807, described how his artillery made a breach in the wall of the town. At first, however, the assaulting party in the darkness of night were unable to find the breach, because *'the enemy had covered it with hides'*.[7]

Today Uruguay still produces hides, and possesses an important leather industry, consisting of many small establishments that make shoes, gloves, and so on. Some of the larger tanneries are owned by Swiss, British, and North American interests.

Metal-working. The metal-working industry is concerned mainly with the final elaboration of a variety of imported semi-manufactures and raw materials, for example, household appliances and kitchen utensils, hinges, nails, screws, bolts, &c. There are a number of small iron foundries, forges, sheet-metal shops, and repair shops. Bodies for lorries are made locally. There is a relatively large industry for the manufacture of fancy jewellery.

Glassware and building materials. Glassware, bricks, and tiles are produced locally in adequate quantities. Limestone and clay are abundant. (The manufacture of cement has been referred to above.)

Electrical appliances. Wireless sets are produced by a company which is under the technical direction of the General Electric Company of New York, and large quantities of imported components are assembled in local factories. Electric lamps for domestic use are manufactured in Montevideo for the various subsidiaries of well-known foreign firms. Refrigerating units and components for electric stoves are imported, and are assembled locally. There is a considerable local manufacture of electric light fittings.

Cigarettes. The many small firms making cigarettes are protected by high import duties and are able to satisfy the local market. Raw tobacco is imported.

TRANSPORT

Railways. Railway construction began in the late 1860's. The gradual extension of the railway system not only assisted the

[7] See Chapter III.

economic development of the country: it also enabled the central Government to deal more rapidly with uprisings in the interior. By 1911 British private enterprise, encouraged in various ways by the Uruguayan authorities (for example, a minimum income was guaranteed), had completed the railway network substantially in its present form. In 1911 the railway mileage in proportion to the area of the republic exceeded that of any other country in the continent. On the whole, British capital was fairly well remunerated, but there was frequent local dissatisfaction with the facilities provided for the transport of crops and cattle, and there were constant complaints that the railways charged excessive rates. With the object of compelling the private railways to reduce their charges, the Government embarked upon a comprehensive programme of highway construction, and took measures to encourage road transport. For instance, motor carriers were granted partial relief from import duties, exemption from certain taxes, and relatively cheap petrol. Moreover, Batlle and his party, being strongly opposed to foreign ownership, drew up several schemes (none of which was practicable) for nationalizing the railways; and the Government acquired or constructed about 600 kilometres of line. These state railways did not represent an integrated system, but constituted a number of small 'feeders' to the British-owned Central Uruguayan Railway. They had no independent access to Montevideo, and they incurred an annual deficit of about 300,000 pesos.

After the conclusion of the Second World War, blocked sterling was utilized for the purchasing of the British railways. The entire network is now state-owned and run by the Administración de los Ferrocarriles del Estado, or AFE.

Four main lines connect the northern and western districts of the republic with Montevideo, but tonnage moving to the port is not balanced by freight in the opposite direction. The total extent of the railways is 1,828 miles, representing a high coverage, by South American standards. The gauge is uniform throughout the country.

The characteristics of the south-eastern section of the railway system are indicated in the following account of a journey during the exceptionally dry summer of 1950, when the writer travelled by rail from Montevideo to Minas. He reported that traffic, once fairly heavy, had dwindled down to a short train of one van, one first-class coach, one second-class coach, and a four-wheeled van for *encomiendas*. Two trains a day were run, one leaving Montevideo in the morning and one in the evening. The service was worked by mixed traffic engines built in Manchester in 1907, and except for a certain amount of modernization they were substantially the same as when they left the works. The traveller's account continues:

The running is quite smart, especially through the local section as far as Peñarol, where the locomotive, carriage, and wagon works of the railway are situated. From Peñarol to Pando, the 'camp' [country] is chiefly devoted to market gardens and orchards, generally irrigated. From Pando to the junction with the Punta del Este lines . . . there is little of interest . . . except for several stone quarries which appear to be working hard. The junction is the site of the works of the State Railway to Punta del Este and is gradually being used more and more for carriage and wagon repairs, the locomotives being dealt with at Peñarol, which works, of course, are now under State ownership.

The character of the 'camp' changes as the line takes a north-easterly direction towards Minas, gradually becoming at first more rolling and later mountainous in a mild way. The line is of a switch-back nature, crossing several valleys, and in fact running up some of these for some distance. These valleys appear to hold the water for a considerable height as both maize and sunflower were in good condition, not only in the valley bottoms but also well up the slopes. The Uruguayan farmer does not waste any land; not only were the hillsides cultivated to a good height, but the railway ground between the track and the fences were also used for growing maize, pumpkin, sweet potato, and melons. . . .

A growing industry in this sector is that of sugar beet. There is a large factory at Montes owned by the Remolachera Azucarera Uruguaya, S.A. (RAUSA). This plant is connected to the main line by a branch about two kilometres long. At many of the stations and halts, and there are quite a few of the latter, sidings have been put in and piles of beet were being loaded. This appears to be a promising industry.

The traffic handled by the passenger train appears to be limited to parcels, lots of milk cans, bags of sweet potatoes, etc., but only in any bulk at points where the route is far away from one of the many paved roads. . . . Minas station . . . is some 30 squares from the town, but a more or less—chiefly less—adequate service of buses connects them together. The town is of typical 'camp' layout with the usual principal Plaza. While lunching at an hotel here, it was extremely noticeable that every half hour or so a large omnibus of modern design left for Montevideo. A visit to the local transport office with its piles of outward and inward parcels, some of them of considerable bulk, and the constant passage of lorries loaded with goods from all over the country, left one with the impression that the railway cannot conceivably make a profit in Uruguay.[8]

Since that account was written, AFE have imported a considerable number of diesel locomotives and other modern equipment, but large deficits have occurred year by year.

Roads. As indicated above, the railways are now meeting with severe competition from road transport, and they are particularly vulnerable in the vicinity of Montevideo, where the road system is more substantial than in the interior. Most rural roads are of earth and are unfit to sustain the increasing traffic of passenger vehicles and heavy lorries. The chief provincial centres are served by fleets of buses, some of which, imported from the United States, are of the luxury Greyhound type. The Uruguayan section of the Pan American Highway runs from Colonia to Montevideo and thence through Treinta y Tres and Melo to Aceguá on the Brazilian frontier.

Municipal transport. At the end of the Second World War the Municipality of Montevideo acquired the city's British-owned tramway company. Tramcars were replaced by trolley-buses. There are also many omnibus services in the capital, most of the vehicles being of North American or British manufacture. A project for the construction of an underground railway has been discussed.

The overcrowding of public transport in Montevideo has been constantly criticized by the press and the general public. This problem 'is aggravated by the two-hour closure of shops and businesses for lunch for which the majority of workers return to their homes. There are thus four traffic peaks a day'.[9]

---

[8] *Review of the River Plate*, 30 March 1950, p. 19.
[9] G.B., Commercial Relations and Exports Dept., *Uruguay*, p. 9.

In 1951 the Municipality raised the minimum bus and tram fare from 8 to 10 centésimos, with the object of applying the 2-centésimo increase to a transport fund, from which would be paid higher wages and the cost of new vehicles. This measure met with such strong opposition that the Municipality were compelled to suspend the new fares. The matter was then put to the popular vote in accordance with a clause in the Constitution which provides that if one-fifth of the total voting population appeals against any measure taken to increase public expenditure, then a plebiscite may be held to decide the issue. At the plebiscite, which took place in July 1951, the proposal to raise the fares was decisively rejected. This referendum was the first of its kind in the history of the country. It was hailed by the weekly newspaper *Marcha* as a healthy example of 'direct democracy' in action. The Municipality were then obliged to obtain the necessary funds by means of a loan and additional taxation.

Shipping. Although Uruguay has such an extensive coastline and such a well-placed port in Montevideo, the Uruguayans have never been a maritime people, and they rely almost entirely on the shipping of foreign nations.

The Port Authority (Administración Nacional de Puertos, or ANP) dates from 1908, in which year the port works of Montevideo were completed.[10] The Government then undertook to operate the port, but permitted private enterprises to continue many of their services. ANP is a public corporation, and in 1932 it began to exercise a monopoly. It runs the port warehouses as well as the principal tugboat, lighterage, and stevedoring services; and it manages the other ports in the country and a small mercantile marine.

The National Institute of Fisheries (SOYP) operates several motorized fishing smacks. ANCAP has a small fleet of tankers and barges. And there are also a number of river craft and small coastal vessels. There are several yacht clubs outside Montevideo, and sailing is a popular sport.

As has been stated, Montevideo is the winter anchorage of the Antarctic whaling flotillas. It is also the only port of call on the South American mainland for ships voyaging to and from

[10] For details of the accommodation in Montevideo see ibid. pp. 6–7.

the Falkland Islands, as the Argentine Government does not allow any direct communication between that British Colony and Argentine ports, which, of course, are much nearer the islands.[11]

Aviation. In such a small country as Uruguay, relatively well served by railways and roads, there is no urgent need for civil aviation. Nevertheless, regular services are provided by Primeras Líneas Uruguayas de Navegación Aérea (PLUNA) between Montevideo and the chief towns of the interior. The present PLUNA company was created in 1944 to take over a former private airline of the same name. Minimum services were fixed by legislation. The original capital of the company consisted of 833,000 pesos subscribed by the state and 167,000 pesos subscribed by the shareholders of the private company. Three directors were to be appointed by the Government and two by the private shareholders. The president of the company was appointed by the Government from among the three state-nominated directors. PLUNA's services have been extended to Brazil, Paraguay, and Bolivia. Well-known foreign airway companies—using the modern airport at Carrasco, on the outskirts of Montevideo—provide regular services connecting Uruguay with the Pacific Coast countries, the United States, and Europe.

There are daily services between Montevideo and Buenos Aires.

[11] Regarding an Argentine-Uruguayan dispute over communications with the Falklands, see Pendle, *Argentina*, pp. 126–7. A substantial trade was already being carried on between Uruguay and the Falklands early in the nineteenth century, one of the pioneers being Samuel Lafone, an English resident of Montevideo (Michael G. Mulhall, *The English in South America* (Buenos Aires, 1878), pp. 338–9).

Chapter IX

FINANCE

BANKING

The Banco de la República was founded in 1896 and is entirely owned by the State. The directors are appointed by the Government. The Bank's issue department is responsible for the country's note issue. Notes may be issued up to the value of the Bank's capital, plus silver holding of 12 million pesos maximum, plus 50 million for rediscounting the papers of the other banks. In 1950 the issue department was further authorized to rediscount certain commercial bills 'relating to trade in merchandise, raw materials, cattle and produce of the country', with the proviso that 'the notes thus issued will be withdrawn from circulation as and when the bills rediscounted are liquidated.'[1]

One of the chief purposes of the Banco de la República has been to provide cheap rural credit. But in the years immediately preceding 1959 its most important function was the supervision of foreign trade and exchange.

The Banco de la República is also a commercial bank, and it transacts about half the commercial bank business in the country.

Proposals for the creation of a separate Central Bank were made in 1962.[2]

In 1912 President Batlle y Ordóñez was authorized by Congress to purchase on behalf of the nation the shares of the privately-owned Banco Hipotecario del Uruguay, which thereby became the State Mortgage Bank. In 1916 the Banco Hipotecario inaugurated a Savings Bank Department, which was immediately popular. In 1921 a law was passed enabling the Banco Hipotecario to grant special loans for the construc-

---

[1] Bank of London & South America, *Fortnightly Review*, 16 December 1950, p. 291. By the end of 1960, however, the volume of rediscounts had risen to 468 million pesos.
[2] Ibid. 27 January 1962, p. 58.

tion of workers' houses. Public employees and private workers enrolled in retirement pension schemes were eligible for these loans. The Bank was also authorized to purchase land, to be subdivided for colonists.

Other state banks are the State Insurance Bank (Banco de Seguros del Estado) and the Postal Savings Bank (Banco Nacional de Ahorro Postal). There are also a number of private domestic and foreign banks, whose credit operations are restricted by law.

INSURANCE

In 1911, on the recommendation (as usual) of President Batlle, the state was granted the monopoly of most classes of insurance, and the Banco de Seguros del Estado was formed, its capital being obtained by a bond issue. On reconsideration, private companies which had been operating before the formation of the Bank were allowed to continue with life, fire, and marine insurance.

A large part of the Bank's re-insurance is effected on the London market.

PUBLIC EXPENDITURE

Government expenditure has risen year by year; but until the end of 1950 inflation was moderate, by Latin American standards. The reasons for the deterioration which occurred after 1950 have been explained by the Economic Commission for Latin America:

> During periods when the terms of trade were very favourable and the volume of foreign trade stood at peak levels—immediately after the [second world] war and during 1950–51—a policy of wage increases, consumer subsidies and development of production could be applied without affecting monetary stability, particularly as the relative rigidity of currency issues had prevented an exaggerated expansion in the money supply, at least until 1950. Moreover, the abundant receipts accruing from duties on foreign trade and the multiple exchange rate system, together with a satisfactory volume of saving, enabled growing public expenditure to be financed without risk of inflation. From 1950 to 1951, the rise in the cost of living . . . was apparently caused by a redistribution of

income in favour of the wage-earning sector and a corresponding increase in consumer demand.

But, since 1952–53, the [favourable] action of the external factors has disappeared; as prices for exports dropped, so costs have risen and, since official social and economic policy have not altered, disequilibria have appeared both in public finance and in the private sector, which was solved by increasing the money supply.[3]

The most important inflationary pressures of domestic origin during the 1950's were a persistent Budget deficit—which became difficult to finance by non-inflationary means—and constant wage increases. (According to the Banco de la República, between 1948 and 1954 wages of workers in 31 trade unions increased by 110 per cent., while the cost-of-living index rose by 58 per cent.) A major factor in government expenditure was the cost of the extensive bureaucracy employed in connexion with the welfare services, &c. But although successive budgetary deficits in themselves constituted a sufficiently serious problem, they did not reveal the full extent of the financial predicament, because much expenditure does not fall within the general Budget. For example, several of the state-owned entities have continually operated at a loss (the total railway deficit from 1949 to 1955 amounted to some 162 million pesos).[4]

REVENUE

Government deficits have been covered periodically by the issuing of internal bonds and by increased borrowing from the banks. Most internal bonds have been taken up by the national pension funds.

Batlle y Ordóñez considered income tax to be a discouragement to personal initiative, so this source of revenue was not introduced until after the Blancos' electoral victory of 1958. Income tax was first levied in Uruguay in 1961.

The system of direct taxation—which is complex—includes taxes on the capital of commercial firms, real estate, industrial and commercial sales, excess profits, tobacco, matches, alco-

[3] U.N., ECLA, *Economic Survey of Latin America, 1954*, p. 196.
[4] Bank of London & South America, *Fortnightly Review*, 29 September 1956, p. 613.

holic beverages, horse-racing, tyres, pharmaceutical products, &c. Stamps have to be purchased as a contribution towards employees' pensions, &c.

When a new budgetary expense is incurred, existing taxes are increased or new taxes are instituted for that special purpose. For example, when the Government decided in 1950 to increase the wages of public servants they simultaneously announced that they would obtain the necessary sum (50 million pesos) by means of a special tax on whisky, entertainments, and other luxuries.

The laws which determine the various proportions in which a person's estate shall be distributed among the surviving members of the family are many and complicated. The laws, decrees, and resolutions which regulate the taxes on inheritance (or death duties) are so numerous and involved that years are liable to elapse before an estate has been finally wound up.

Customs duties are a major source of revenue, but of course they are liable to decline in amount under the influence of import restrictions, or of a falling off in foreign trade for some other reason.

FOREIGN INVESTMENT

Uruguay's public services were to a very large extent developed by means of foreign capital, but this dependence on foreign funds was always disliked and resented by many Uruguayans. In 1907 Batlle wrote: 'We can make great progress during the next twenty years if we have honest government and especially if we are less generous in handing out money to foreign corporations.'[5] In 1911, when the tramway workers had won an increase in wages by means of a strike, Batlle exclaimed:

Without this strike this wage increase would have continued to go, together with the rest of the abundant profits, to London and Berlin to swell the pockets of British and German shareholders. Now it remains here to be distributed among our own people.[6]

---

[5] Roberto B. Giudici, *Batlle y el Batllismo* (Montevideo, 1928), p. 383.
[6] *El Día* (Montevideo), 25 May 1911.

In 1913 British capital investments in Uruguay totalled £46,145,393, comprising £25,552,548 in Government Bonds and £20,592,845 in economic enterprises (of which last figure, the amount of £15,352,963 was invested in the railways). On these investments an average of 4·6 per cent. was paid in interest. In 1945 British investments totalled £43,819,938, producing an average interest of 2·9 per cent.

The Uruguayan Government then utilized blocked sterling, which had accumulated during the war, to purchase all the British utilities except the Montevideo Gas and Dry Dock Company (which was the oldest of them all). By a financial agreement signed in 1947 it was provided that of the sterling balances then in existence, there should be released immediately and unconditionally a sum of £1 million and, at the end of twelve months, a further amount of £700,000. £120,000 was made available for expenses of the Uruguayan Embassy in London and £130,000 for scholarships for Uruguayans in the United Kingdom. £4 million was reserved as part of the purchase price of the British-owned railways, and £3 million for the purchase of public utilities in general. £6 million was to be used for the reduction of the Uruguayan external debt, or in payment for the railways, and a further £1½ million was to be released in equal annual instalments. The price of the tramways was subsequently fixed at £1,814,000; that of the Montevideo waterworks at £3 million, and the price of the railways at £17,150,000. In 1949 the value of British investments had fallen to £26,624,198 (providing in that year an average interest of 4·7 per cent.).

In normal times, the influx of foreign capital is relatively small, but the incoming amount increased for a while after the accession to power of President Perón in Argentina (1946) and, again, after the outbreak of war in Korea (1950) when very large quantities of dollars, gold, and other currencies were sent or repatriated to Uruguay for safe keeping. In his review of the year ending 31 December 1950, the chairman of the Bank of London & South America remarked: 'It is evident that during the present period of unsettled international affairs, Uruguay is regarded as one of the countries least affected. This fact and the absence of political unrest make it attractive to those seeking a safe refuge for their funds.'[7]

[7] *The Times*, 9 March 1951. The United Nations have published a convenient study of the history of foreign investment in Uruguay and related matters: U.N., Dept. of Economic and Social Affairs, *Foreign Capital in Latin America* (New York, 1955), pp. 139–43. The sub-headings in this section are: External Public Debt; Foreign Business Investments; Industrial Distribution of Business Investments; Entry and Status of Foreign Capital; Exchange Control; Taxation; and Government Participation in Economic Activities.

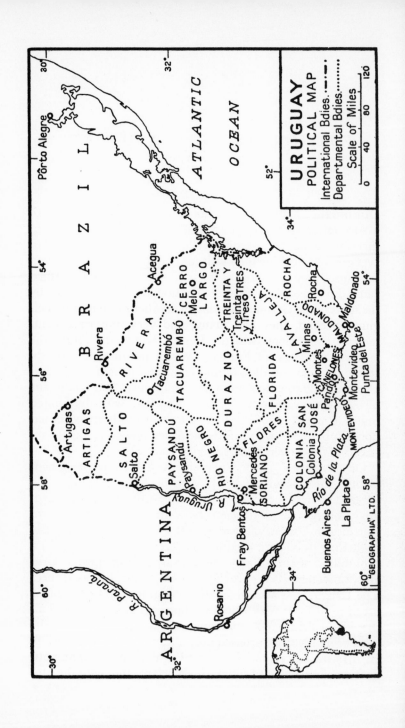

Chapter X

FOREIGN RELATIONS AND PARTY POLITICS

FOREIGN RELATIONS

DURING the First World War the Uruguayans were faced with a succession of international problems. Month by month, therefore, under the pressure of events, they had to define with ever greater precision their attitude and their intentions. From the outset they had motives for sympathizing with the Allied cause. First, as citizens of a small nation, they were shocked by the news of the German invasion of another small nation, Belgium. Second, they had many, and very important commercial connexions with the United Kingdom. Third, the cultural influence of France was still paramount. Fourth, Italian settlers and their families now constituted a considerable and valuable element in the community. And finally, the Uruguayans were aware of their close ties with the United States as members of the Pan-American brotherhood of nations. Public goodwill towards the Allies, however, was always ahead of the Government's pronouncements.

On 4 August 1914 the Government issued a decree of neutrality. Three days later they published a list of rules providing for the maintenance and safeguarding of neutrality in Uruguay. These rules established: (a) a time-limit for belligerent warships in Uruguayan waters; (b) a limit to the amount of re-fuelling to be permitted to belligerent warships; and (c) a prohibition against the use of radio by foreign ships in Uruguayan waters. As the war progressed, neutrality weakened. The Uruguayans accepted with good grace the British black list of local firms with whom trading was forbidden, and although the British restrictions on trade were detrimental to the local economy, they aroused only a minimum of indignation. In 1917 the Government protested against the German notification of unrestricted submarine warfare, and, with the support of the entire press, formally announced their approval of Washington's rupture of diplomatic relations with Germany. When the United States declared war, the Government expressed their recognition of the justice of the decision. As Uruguay had suffered no act of aggression, however, neutrality was re-affirmed. When Brazil ceased to be neutral in June 1917, Uruguay offered its support to the extent of declaring that 'no American country, which in defence of its own rights should find itself in a state of war with nations of other continents, will be treated as a belligerent'.[1] Several other Latin American countries followed this lead. The Government still hoped that all the republics would then agree to some form of concerted action; but in October 1917, no such agreement having been reached, they decided to delay no longer. They severed diplomatic relations with Germany and revoked their own neutrality decrees with regard to the Allies. They ordered the arrest of the captains of German ships anchored in Montevideo harbour, because the regulations concerning radio equipment had been violated, and they leased the eight German vessels to the Emergency Fleet Corporation of the United States. At this time they also accorded credits to the Allies to facilitate the maintenance of supplies of Uruguayan pastoral and agricultural products.

Between the wars Uruguay was a conscientious member of the League of Nations and, as befitted a buffer state, was on friendly terms with its neighbours. During the Second World War, however, tension developed between Montevideo and Buenos Aires. Many Uruguayans disliked the undemocratic features of the wartime régimes in Argentina, while the Argentine military and nationalist leaders resented Uruguay's readiness to co-operate with the United States. In the Second World War, as in the First, the Uruguyan Government made it quite clear that their sympathies lay with the Allies. In December 1939 the German warship *Graf Spee* was compelled to seek refuge in Montevideo harbour and, as the Government refused to allow it to make an extended stay, it was scuttled by its crew in the estuary of the Río de la Plata. The stranded

---

[1] *Memoria de relaciones exteriores, 1916–18*, pp. 439–40, quoted in P. A. Martin, *Latin America and the War* (Baltimore, Johns Hopkins Press, 1925), p. 363.

German sailors found that Argentina was a congenial refuge. The German authorities at once complained that the Uruguayans had behaved in an unfriendly manner, and their Embassy at Montevideo, by encouraging the dissemination of Nazi propaganda, provoked the Government to arrest a number of pro-Nazis. Uruguay then agreed to establish naval and air bases for the defence of the Americas and accepted the North American offer of financial and technical assistance in this undertaking. In January 1942, one month after the attack on Pearl Harbour, Uruguay severed relations with the Axis Powers. The Blanco leader, Dr. Luis Alberto de Herrera, protested against all these anti-Axis actions. He regarded the German threat to Latin America as negligible, but considered that there was a real danger of North American dominance of the whole continent. He therefore desired that Uruguay should remain strictly neutral. In this respect his policy was identical with that of the nationalists of Argentina, among whom he had many close friends. During the whole of this period, and subsequently, the behaviour of the Argentine nationalists and of many Argentine officers created the impression not only that they expected but also that they hoped that the Axis would win the war. One small incident will serve to illustrate the different attitudes of the Uruguayan and Argentine authorities at this time. When Charlie Chaplin's film *The Great Dictator* arrived in the Río de la Plata, it was banned in Argentina but was freely shown in Uruguay. Indeed, thousands of Argentines travelled across the river in special excursions to see the film in the cinemas of Colonia and Montevideo.

The Uruguayans are usually careful not to cause too much offence to Argentina. After the war, however, the newspapers and radio frequently criticized President Perón and his supporters, Argentine publicists retaliated by suggesting that Uruguay was a centre of Communist intrigue or a satellite of the United States, or both. Meanwhile the Uruguayans doggedly offered asylum to political refugees from Argentina. These refugees were not necessarily democrats. Among them, for instance, was General Perón's former colleague, Miguel Miranda.

Subsequent developments in the relations between Monte-

video and Buenos Aires have been referred to above, in connexion with the tourist trade.[2]

For many years relations with Brazil have been particularly
amicable. The Colorados, who for so long governed Uruguay,
always inclined towards Brazil. In the nineteenth century they
admired the progressive policy of Brazil's Dom Pedro II and
the liberal institutions that he inaugurated. The Brazilians,
moreover, even when they occupied the Banda Oriental, respected the nation's sovereignty. In recent times Brazil has
been served by a number of exceptionally able diplomats.

Year by year, as the inter-American system takes shape,
Uruguay—not being strong enough to defend itself—gives its
support to plans for mutual defence in the Americas. In 1946
the Government even proposed collective action by the nations of the hemisphere against any American country which
might default on its international obligations or deny to its
own people 'the elementary rights of man and citizen'.[3]

Uruguay's representatives have always taken an active part
in the United Nations. After the outbreak of war in Korea they
advocated the strengthening of the authority of the General
Assembly and maintained that because of the failure of the
Great Powers to prevent war the small nations were now
called upon to make an important contribution to the organiz-
ing of international security. In 1950 the Uruguayan delegation to the United Nations proposed that the definition of
international aggression should be widened to include indirect
aggression 'such as the creation by any Power of subversive
agencies in foreign countries with the object of undermining
those countries' institutions'. The resumption of full diplomatic relations with Spain was opposed because 'in 1946 the
United Nations agreed that the Government of General
Franco had been established with the help and intervention of
the Axis powers and was of a totalitarian nature, and nothing
has happened in the meantime to alter the case'. The Uruguayan spokesman argued, furthermore, that Spain was not
fit to become a member of the United Nations, because

---

[2] See above, p. 57.
[3] Austin F. Macdonald, *Latin American Politics and Government* (New York,
Crowell, 1949), p. 464.

General Franco's party had placed all Spanish trade unions and all education under the absolute control of the state and had closed the frontiers to a large number of exiles. 'A government of that kind would be ill qualified to participate in the work of the specialized organizations of the United Nations which deal with questions concerning labour, culture, and refugees.' During discussions on the former Italian colonies the Uruguayan delegation insisted that the wishes of the local population should be respected and demanded the rejection of the thesis

that independence should be denied a nation because of its lack of economic resources, the smallness of its territory, the backwardness of its social institutions or its educational deficiencies. Any plan for incorporating Eritrea in a federation of states or in a customs union should only be accepted if it were approved by the inhabitants of the land. Should the people not yet be technically competent to take an advanced political decision of that sort, it would be the duty of the United Nations to promote technical training in the country to enable them eventually to do so.

The Uruguayans held, likewise, that no régime should be imposed upon Jerusalem unless it were freely accepted by the local population. In reference to full employment, the Uruguayan delegation expressed the conviction of their Government that 'nowadays it is impossible to conceive of individual liberty unless it has the economic support of a guaranteed, permanent, and remunerative job for every able-bodied man in conditions appropriate to the proper fulfilment of the human personality'.[4] It is evident, therefore, that the Uruguayans have transported into the sphere of international deliberations the convictions which, since the year 1903, have determined the social and economic development of their own country.

One of the advantages enjoyed by a small buffer state situated between two powerful neighbours is that it need not waste its resources in maintaining a large number of men under arms. There is no conscription in Uruguay, and the people have little respect for their army, air force, and navy.

[4] 'El Uruguay en la Quinta Asamblea General de las Naciones Unidas', *Marcha*, 12 January 1951.

When the Chief of General Staff was asked what inducements the state offered to obtain recruits, he replied:

None whatever. The soldiers live with their wives in our married
quarters. Their children grow up in that atmosphere, helping their
father to clean his equipment and don his uniform. They live
happily there, and the boys quite naturally follow on in their
father's profession.

He added: 'We have no armaments industry in Uruguay, and
therefore we have no military secrets.'

PARTY POLITICS

Uruguay is one of the youngest republics in the New World,
but its political life is dominated by two of the oldest political
parties. The Colorados and the Blancos came into existence
during the struggle for national independence 100 years ago.
At that time the population was divided between those two
camps, and today most Uruguayans are either Colorados or
Blancos 'from birth'. Although Uruguayan politicians during
the past fifty or sixty years have been susceptible to the influence of the latest ideologies, and although many attempts have
been made to form new parties of the types that have arisen in
other countries, the political life of the republic is still contained within the Colorado-Blanco framework, and the proposed new parties have not prospered. In practice, any politi-
cian aspiring to popular success has had to make his career as a
member of one of the two traditional groups, and Batlle himself was careful to carry out his revolutionary policy from within the Colorado fraternity. Innumerable personal variations
have occurred in both groups since the days of Rivera and
Oribe, but the mass of the population still cast their votes
either for the Colorados or for the Blancos.

The Colorados and Blancos are not animated by opposed
ideologies: their allegiance is to persons and traditions, and
the difference between their politics is so slight that it has never
been satisfactorily defined. Members of the principal Blanco
faction (the Herrera Nationalists) even claim, humorously,
that although they cannot call themselves Batllistas they have
inherited the large overcoat that Batlle invariably wore during

his political campaigns and are therefore his true descendants. The Blancos are often identified as conservatives and the Colorados as liberals, but there are liberals and conservatives in both groups, and in Congress the respective right wings and left wings frequently combine and vote together. It can be argued that the Blancos are Catholics and the Colorados agnostics, but there are many good Catholics among the Colorados and many Blancos are indifferent to religion. It is said that the Blancos are less cosmopolitan than their political rivals and more imbued with the national traditions, but the Colorados also pay homage to those traditions and they cannot be accused of having failed to sustain the prestige of the nation. The spirit of the Blancos may appear to be more in harmony with that of the nineteenth-century gauchos, but the founder of the Colorado party, Rivera, was himself a gaucho. Neither party has the support of any particular social class. Neither of them has a clear programme. It would be accurate to state, however, that the Blancos are less willing than the Colorados to adopt social and economic innovations and that they appeal to the older elements of the population, which are of Spanish origin, rather than to the more recently arrived Italian and Central European elements.

It might have been expected that the two great parties would alternate in government. For more than ninety years, however, the heads of State were Colorados, and after the suppression of the insurrection during Batlle's first term of office the Blancos democratically fulfilled the function, so to say, of 'Her Majesty's Opposition'. Nevertheless, although the Blancos were out of office for so long, their two factions (the Hertera Nationalists and the Independent Nationalists) generally had the support of about 40 per cent. of the voters, and the Blancos at last won a majority of seats in both houses of Congress in 1958.

There are important subdivisions within both the major groups. Even in the time of José Batlle y Ordóñez several crises occurred in the Colorado group, and factions broke away from his leadership over questions such as that of the plural executive.[5] A further subdivision took place during the presidency

[5] See above, p. 33.

of Gabriel Terra, whose dictatorship was unacceptable to many Colorados.[6] During elections, however, the various Colorado factions usually composed their differences. The principal split in the Blanco Party also occurred during the Terra dictatorship, when the Independent Nationalists broke away from Dr Luis Alberto de Herrera's Nationalists, as a protest against the latter's collaboration with the President. Thus the Colorado and the Blanco parties both broke internally on the same issue.

At the 1950 elections, as usual, three Colorado factions nominated presidential candidates. The group headed by the outgoing President, Luis Batlle Berres (a nephew of José Batlle y Ordóñez), nominated Martínez Trueba, who had the support of Batlle Berre's newspaper, *Acción*. A second group of Batllistas, backed by Batlle y Ordóñez's three sons, Lorenzo, Rafael, and César, and by their newspaper, *El Día*, nominated Mayo Gutiérrez. The third group, the Independent Colorados, had as their candidate Blanco Acevedo, who personally was perhaps rather more conservative in outlook than the others. Although Herrera again polled more votes than any of the three Colorados, the aggregate Colorado poll exceeded that of the Nationalists by 178,620. The Colorados, therefore, won the elections, and their leading candidate, Andrés Martínez Trueba, took office as President of the republic on 1 March 1951. At these elections 53 Colorados and 38 Blancos (Nationalists and Independent Nationalists together) were elected to the Chamber of Deputies, out of a total of 99. Of the 30 senators elected, 17 were Colorados and 12 Blancos. In July 1951 the Batllistas and the Herrerista Nationalists signed the pact on constitutional reform.[7]

The Second World War produced considerable acrimony in internal politics, and the two major parties disagreed more vehemently on foreign affairs than on any domestic issue. Dr Herrera's opposition to the Government's pro-Allied policy during the war is mentioned above. The majority of Colorados maintained that the Nationalist leader's uncompromising 'neutral' attitude was an indication of his pro-Axis sympathies, just as, in their opinion, his refusal to denounce the Franco

[6] See above, pp. 34–35.   [7] See above, p. 7.

régime in Spain was proof of his Fascist tendencies. During the war the dissolution of *Herrerismo* was demanded in the name of patriotism and democracy; but it was perhaps Communist propagandists rather than Colorados who issued the slogans against 'nazi-fasci-nipofalanjo-herrerismo' which were plastered on the walls of Montevideo streets. Propaganda of that kind certainly was repugnant to the mass of the population, by whom Dr Herrera was never regarded as the Uruguayan equivalent of Hitler, Mussolini, or Franco.

For fifty years the workpeople were championed by the ruling political party. It is not surprising, therefore, that trade unions should have been slow to develop and that Communism should be weak in Uruguay. Recently trade unions have increased in importance in the towns, and their representatives now usually act on behalf of the workers in labour disputes, which are taken before the government-appointed Instituto Nacional de Trabajo for settlement. Under the influence of post-war inflation, strikes have become more frequent. In most instances they have been brought to an end by the granting of the workers' demands for higher wages, as the Colorado Government consistently favoured labour rather than the employers.

The most powerful labour organization is the Unión General de Trabajadores (UGT), which is affiliated to the reputedly Marxist-dominated international Confederación de Trabajadores de América-Latina (CTAL); but a large number of workers belong to the non-Communist Confederación Sindical del Uruguay (CSU), which is affiliated to the CTAL's rival, the Organización Regional Interamericana de Trabajadores (ORIT). Some of the more important unions remain unaffiliated to any international federation.

Although Communists have played a part in the running of certain unions, Communism has nevertheless made little progress. At the end of the Second World War a company was formed in Montevideo to publish Spanish translations of Communist books, and for a while the bookstalls and kiosks were flooded with the works of Marx, Lenin, and Stalin. The company was said to be financed with local funds. The Uruguayan market, however, was too small to justify such an ambitious undertaking, and when General Perón came to power in Argentina the principal export market for these publications was closed, and the venture therefore terminated.

Uruguay is predominantly a bourgeois country. Until now, the gradual socialism introduced by Batlle y Ordóñez has satisfied the requirements of the urban working-class population and has thus prevented the growth of Communism in the accustomed quarters. The great problem for the future will be to find some means of extending to the rural districts the relative well-being which exists in Montevideo. This, in other terms, is the problem with which Artigas was concerned at the beginning of the last century: how shall a more just and healthy balance be attained in the life of the country as a whole? Today, the need for this adjustment is widely recognized and, as noted in previous chapters, it is being met to some extent by the setting up of factories in provincial towns, the provision of electric power, and the improvement of transport and communications.

Chapter XI

CULTURE

DURING the colonial period there was no literature of the Banda Oriental. The gauchos improvised verses, which they sang to the accompaniment of their own guitars; and love-songs in popular metres—a heritage of Spanish folklore—were current. But the ballads and songs were not recorded in writing. The first printing-press ever set up in the Banda was brought to Montevideo by the British invaders in 1807 and was removed when they departed a few months later. During the wars of the early nineteenth century the forms of popular poetry were used to express in simple, sometimes crude, language the hatred of the opposing factions and the glory of revolution and independence. One notable poet who imitated gaucho verse for patriotic purposes was a Montevideo bartender and revolutionary soldier, Bartolomé Hidalgo (1788–1822).

The main entertainments in Montevideo were dancing and cockfighting. There was one small theatre, which was visited by Alexander Caldcleugh in 1821:

In the evening I attended the play, and was introduced by one of the governor's staff to all the most celebrated beauties in the city, who were extremely polite, and, according to custom, pressed me to eat more sweetmeats than I could have wished. The theatre was small and ill arranged; the actors, it may be supposed, not of the best. One of the farces exhibited, *El Inglez con Splin*, gave rise to many good natured, yet witty observations from the ladies, on our national character.[1]

Another British traveller noted that in 1842 the theatre was 'small and mean; but [he added] a new one is now building which will be considerably larger than the theatre royal in the Haymarket'.[2] This new theatre—the Solís—was inaugurated

[1] Alexander Caldcleugh, *Travels in South America* (London, Murray, 1825), i. 122–3.
[2] W. Whittle, *Journal of a Voyage to the River Plate* (Manchester, 1846), p. 68.

in 1856 and was one of the finest in South America. (It is still in use today.) Richard Burton remarked that in 1868 the principal theatrical company was 'the Compañía de Zarzuela, a Spanish buffo . . . [of] purely Iberian style'. By that time there were three theatres besides the Solís, and 'the Great American Circus'.[3]

As the spirit of national independence developed, romanticism became fashionable among those who had literary pretensions. Romanticists such as Victor Hugo, Alfred de Musset, Lamartine, and Byron were adopted as models. But throughout the short history of Uruguayan literature and art there have been two rival points of view, and this dualism still exists. On the one hand are the groups who follow the latest Eurolean literary and artistic fashions. On the other hand are those who produce regional verse, drama, and paintings. To some extent, however, the nineteenth-century romanticists united these two tendencies.

Romanticism seemed made to fit [Latin] American temperaments and conditions. It stood for freedom, for individualism, and for emotional intensity. It exalted nature as the source of poetic inspiration. It sought for its subject matter phases of life remote in space or in time from the great centres of contemporary civilization.[4]

The Latin American romanticists conformed to a European pattern, but they chose to write on Latin American themes. Thus Uruguay's first notable writer, Juan Zorilla de San Martín (1855–1931), although he wrote under the influence of European romantic literature, was at the same time a fervid nationalist concentrating on the legends, history, and heroes of his homeland.

Zorilla was not only a romanticist in his writing, he was romantic in behaviour and even in appearance, with his abundant mass of hair and his chiselled profile. In 1879 he became known to the general public by reciting a patriotic ode of his

---

[3] *Letters from the Battle-fields of Paraguay*, pp. 123–4. For the history of Montevideo's theatres see Horacio Arredondo, *Civilización del Uruguay* (Montevideo, 1951), i. 243–9.

[4] E. Herman Hespelt, ed., *An Outline History of Spanish American Literature*, 2nd ed. (New York, Crofts, 1949), pp. 45–46.

own composition, *La Leyenda Patria*, and thereafter, during the remainder of his long life, he recited that poem at almost every national ceremony that he attended. Indeed, in 1880 an unkind commentator remarked that a certain ceremony was unique, because on this occasion 'Dr Zorrilla de San Martín did *not* recite the *Leyenda Patria*'. Zorrilla's masterpiece in verse was *Tabaré*, an epic of the indigenous Indians. His greatest work in prose was *La Epopeya de Artigas*, which was an effective vindication of Uruguay's hero. Zorrilla is considered to have symbolized a national renaissance. He was showered with honours and eulogies. A contemporary of Zorilla's was Eduardo Acevedo Díaz (1851–1924) who wrote historical novels on Uruguayan gaucho themes.

Towards the end of the nineteenth century in Uruguay, as in the other Latin American republics, a *modernista* reaction arose against romanticism. Political conditions were gradually becoming more stable. Economic progress, stimulated by foreign investment, helped to increase the wealth of a small upper class, thereby providing greater opportunity for leisure. And so a genuine aesthetic movement became possible. Once again, the principal influence was French, the fashionable models being Gautier, Baudelaire, Sully Prudhomme, Leconte de Lisle, &c.

A new factor, however, had already begun to affect the outlook of Latin American writers: namely, the ever increasing power of the United States, whose great material development contrasted with the backwardness of the southern republics. Earlier, the Argentine educator Sarmiento and his Uruguayan disciple Varela[5] had preached that Latin America should take the United States as its model,[6] but some of their successors now felt the need to withstand the pressure from the north. This reaction against so-called *Nordomanía* was expressed with particular force by the Uruguayan modernist José Enrique Rodó (1872–1917).

[5] See above, pp. 28–29.
[6] Alberto Zum Felde, *Indice crítico de la literatura hispano-americana* (Mexico, 1954), p. 291. Zum Felde provides a useful analysis of Rodó's work. There is a copious literature on this subject. See, for example, the special issue of *Número* (nos. 6, 7 and 8, January-June 1950), published on the fiftieth anniversary of the publication of *Ariel*, and Emir Rodríguez Monegal, *José E. Rodó en el novecientos* (Montevideo, 1950).

In his slender masterpiece *Ariel* (1900) Rodó stressed the inadequacy of mere technical progress and the pursuit of wealth and power. He reaffirmed the value of the humanist and classic traditions inherited from Europe's Greek and Latin civilizations. And he called upon the people of Latin America to create their own 'aristocracy of the spirit'. Rodó's conception of a Latin American aristocracy of the spirit was rather refined, far removed from the life of the gaucho and the indigenous Indian, just as his style of writing was inclined to be precious and overwrought, lacking the robustness of the people to whom he wished to appeal. Nevertheless, '*Ariel* was widely read and discussed, for many years, from Mexico and the Antilles to Argentina and Chile, and *Arielismo* replaced *Nordomanía*, at least among many of the young'.[7] Today the book is still referred to as the ethical Bible of Latin America. It was certainly one of the earliest Latin American statements of anxiety about the influence of the materialistic features of North American democracy (personified in the book as Caliban, an evil to be resisted). In spite of the fact, however, that the defeat of Spain by the United States in the Cuban war of 1898 had caused alarm in Latin America,[8] Rodó himself was not concerned with the danger of North American political hegemony over the Western hemisphere; nor had he envisaged the possibility of 'dollar imperialism'—though his readers imagined that they found such implications in his text. His preoccupations, in reality, were mainly aesthetic. Rodó's contemporary, Carlos Vaz Ferreira, dedicated himself to bringing modernism into Uruguayan education and philosophy.

This period—the turn of the century—was the golden age of Uruguayan literature (while being also, as we have seen, the time of Batlle's vigorous campaign for social and economic reforms). Among the most talented modernists was Julio Herrera y Reissig (1875–1910), who formed a group of 'Bohemian' poets and had considerable influence on Latin American poetry in general. And within the modernist movement there developed another new group, the realists. Their work was

---

[7] Pedro Henríquez Ureña, *Literary Currents in Hispanic America* (Harvard University Press, 1949), pp. 179–80.

[8] Carlos Real de Azúa, *Número*, nos. 6, 7, and 8, 1950, p. 35.

regional, naturalistic, and colloquial, representing 'headlong flight from the ivory tower into the midst of local environments'. The outstanding Uruguayan realist was a playwright, Florencio Sánchez (1875–1910), who wrote rough-and-ready plays in Río de la Plata settings. Florencio Sánchez is still the best known of South American dramatists. Novelists and short story writers such as Horacio Quiroga (1878–1937) dealt with local rural life.

In recent decades the most distinguished poets have been women. Except in one instance, their verse is personal, having little connexion with contemporary trends. María Eugenia Vaz Ferreira (1875–1924) wrote mystical verse. Delmira Agustini (1886–1914) came of a wealthy family. She was unhappily married and was killed by her husband. Her poems, erotic and mystical, were compared by Rubén Darío to those of Santa Teresa herself. By contrast Juana de Ibarbourou (b. 1895) has had a simple and happy married life. Her poetry, which is immensely popular, is uncomplicated and sensuous. Sara de Ibáñez belongs to the school of Spanish poets of the 1930's. Outstanding male poets of the present time are Carlos Sábat Ercasty, who is described as the Uruguayan Walt Whitman, and the metaphysical poet Emilio Oribe.

By an odd coincidence modern French poetry is linked with Uruguay: Lautréamont, Laforgue, and Supervielle were all born in Montevideo.

Among leading modern writers of short stories are Francisco Espínola, Enrique Amorim, and Juan José Morosoli. They have all written of rural villages and the remnants of gaucho life in the interior of the republic.

The market for books is small, and most authors are obliged to finance their own publications, though the Ministry of Public Instruction assists by offering prizes and by purchasing a certain number of copies.

Uruguay's best-known painters are Juan Manuel Blanes, who produced meticulously true-to-life historical scenes, Pedro Figari, and Torres García. Pedro Figari (1861–1938) is one of the greatest of South American artists, and his canvases fetch high prices today. They are immediately recognizable, those softly coloured, impressionistic rural scenes: country folk dancing in a patio, or seated beneath an *ombú* tree listening to a guitarist, or grouped stiffly in a provincial drawing-room. Figari's colouring is quite distinctive. He used large quantities of white in his work, and thereby he managed to capture the soft tones of the Río de la Plata twilight. He avoided the clear light and hard shadows of daytime, and chose the gentle evening, when sun and moon are both in the sky, when there are no shadows, and when men and women in nostalgic mood relax after the day's work. An admirer spoke to Figari about the magic of twilight pervading his pictures, and the artist replied: 'It is the light of recollection'. Figari's art is very personal, but it is also very Uruguayan, typical of a land without excessive summers or winters, bland and mild. J. Torres García (1874–1944) was an experimental painter, aiming to create a new American art under the influence of modern international movements.

Elementary education is free and compulsory in Uruguay. Therefore—although the number of schools in the rural districts is inadequate, and there is a shortage of teachers[9]—the rate of illiteracy is lower than in most Latin American countries. The exact extent of illiteracy, however, is disputed. In 1956 the Committee for Complete Literacy announced an illiteracy figure of 3 per cent. in the 15–50 age group; but a UNESCO publication a little while earlier had quoted an estimate of 15–20 per cent. It has been suggested that the discrepancy was the result of the higher northern hemisphere definition of literacy.[10]

Secondary and technical schools and the University of Montevideo (which is one of the largest in Latin America) are likewise open to all, free of cost.

The technical schools are grouped together to form the Universidad de Trabajo (Labour University), which is a dependency of the University of Montevideo. Some of these

---

[9] The training of teachers in Uruguay is the subject of an interesting study by Ligando Chávez: 'Formación de Profesores en Algunos Paises de América: Uruguay', *Revista Ecuatoriana de Educación* (Quito), January-April 1953, pp. 13–127.

[10] *Hispanic American Report*, November 1956, p. 499.

schools are rural, specializing in training for agricultural and pastoral occupations. The urban technical schools teach such subjects as engineering and architecture.

After finishing secondary studies, a student must spent two years in 'preparatory courses' before entering the University of Montevideo. Zum Felde has complained that the university is merely a *fábrica de profesionales*, a factory to produce professional men; that the students' only aim is to pass their examinations and obtain their certificates; and that no one goes there simply in search of enlightenment.[11] But this complaint becomes less justified year by year, especially as the Faculty of Humanities and Sciences now offers a wide choice of courses. All higher education is concentrated in the capital; but in conformity with the general recognition of the need for developing the interior of the republic, proposals have been discussed for decentralizing university education by creating faculties in provincial towns such as Salto and Paysandú.

Employees in most of the government departments and the administrative staff in most of the public corporations attend their offices for half days only. Junior public servants are thus able to continue their studies at the university during the considerable spare time that is available to them.

The National Library in Montevideo is now installed in a new building. Its books are mostly modern. The Historical Museum is rich in local material and has been ably and lovingly organized by the historian, Juan Pivel Devoto, in two beautiful colonial houses, the Casa de Rivera and the Casa de Lavalleja, in Montevideo.

As the Uruguayans are such a literate people, newspapers are widely read; and as the country is small in area and has no great mountain ranges or other natural obstacles to transport, the Montevideo newspapers can be distributed in all except the remotest regions on the day of publication, with the result that provincial papers have an insignificant circulation. The dependence of the provinces on the Montevideo press is yet another indication of the extent (frequently mentioned in the

[11] Zum Felde, *Proceso intelectual del Uruguay* (Montevideo, 1930), Book III, Chapter I.

present book) to which the capital dominates the interior.

In no other country of South America does such a degree of imbalance exist in the organization and significance of the press. . . . The whole historical emphasis on Montevideo at the expense of other cities in the country discourages any effort to set up independent and vigorous papers in the interior. A centralized form of government means that political news and inspiration emanate largely from the capital; and the press of the *campo* reflects the lack of that source of journalistic nourishment. The contrast in circulation and advertising potentials between Montevideo and other cities of the country is obvious and no less apparent is the fact that the financial resources to maintain even a 'political' paper, which does not depend primarily on either advertising or circulation, are not so easily found outside the capital.[12]

Montevideo's newspapers are political rather than commercial enterprises, and just as individuals belong to one or other of the political factions 'from birth', so do they automatically buy the newspaper which represents the appropriate point of view. The most famous daily paper (though no longer the most influential) is *El Día*, founded by José Batlle y Ordóñez in 1886, and still controlled by his one surviving son. A second Colorado faction finds its outlook expressed in *Acción*, owned mainly by Batlle's nephew Luis Batlle Berres. *Acción* gained in importance during the presidencies of Batlle Berres (1947–51) and his successor Martínez Trueba, whose candidacy the paper supported. *El Diario* and *La Mañana* reflect the opinions of the so-called 'Independent' and more conservative branch of the Colorados who broke away from Batlle y Ordóñez on the issue of the *Colegiado*.[13] The Blanco daily *El Debate* represents the right-wing 'Nationalist' point of view of the *Herreristas*. *Tribuna* is of a similar tendency. The newspapers of the more moderately conservative 'Independent Nationalists' are *El País* (morning) and *El Plata* (evening). *El Bien Público* is the Catholic paper, with a very small circulation.[14]

[12] Fitzgibbon, *Uruguay*, pp. 185–6.   [13] See above, p. 13.
[14] A reliable estimate of the circulation of the principal newspapers in 1962 was as follows:

El Día, 50,000	*Tribuna*, 25,000
Acción, 20,000	*El País*, 70,000
El Diario, 150,000	*El Plata*, 50,000
La Mañana, 40,000 Sundays, 25,000 week days	*El Bien Público*, 7,000
El Debate, 10,000	

The sports pages are an important feature of the Montevideo press, a large amount of space being devoted to football. The Uruguayans are proud of their success in international football. The game was first played in Uruguay at the end of the nineteenth century by British residents and the crews of British warships visiting Montevideo. The first enclosed football ground was constructed by the tramway company in 1900. In 1930 the Centenario Stadium, with accommodation for 80,000 spectators, was inaugurated at Montevideo. In 1950, at Rio de Janeiro, the Uruguayans won the world football championship for the fourth time. The Government sent an official aircraft to Brazil to bring the triumphant team home, and proclaimed a national holiday to celebrate the victory. Basket-ball, swimming, rowing, yachting, cycling, and tennis are also popular sports. In the 1890's a group of British residents made the first golf course at Punta Carreta, Montevideo, and there are now golf links at several of the seaside ports. Pelota, brought to Uruguay by Spanish colonists, is a traditional game of the country, but it cannot compare with football or basket-ball in popularity.

Both an official broadcasting organization and private commercial stations operate in Uruguay. The Servicio Oficial de Difusión Radio-eléctrica (SODRE) is financed by the Ministry of Public Instruction. It transmits no advertisements, and it broadcasts news, music, and cultural programmes only.

It has been mentioned above that the circulation of the Catholic newspaper, *El Bien Público*, is very small. Uruguay is a Catholic country, but the Uruguayans nowadays are not a religious people.

It is true that in the early decades of the nineteenth century European visitors invariably went to look at the cathedral and remarked on the religious processions. Whittle observed that when the ladies attended Mass in the cathedral

they always come prepared with a nice little carpet, which a servant, mostly a black girl, spreads upon the floor. When they are tired of kneeling, or the forms of the service permit. they have a way of reclining at their ease somewhat in the Turkish fashion, anon casting a few lightning-like glances around them, to see if any

Cavaliero of their acquaintance is present. About eleven on the Sunday morning the floor of the Cathedral presents a very gay appearance, this being the *misa* which the *élite* make a point of attending.

And this visitor added:

Saints' days occur very frequently; they are more observed than the Sunday: in fact, most of the shops are open on that day. The pomp, processions, and ceremonies of the Roman Catholic ritual can be but faintly conceived as practised in England. Here they almost out-Herod Herod; fireworks, illuminations, bonfires, cannon, all contribute to the display. Formerly there were many convents, but at the revolution they were suppressed.[15]

The general indifference to the Catholic faith which prevails today can be explained largely by the fact that the Banda Oriental was occupied by the Spaniards for only a relatively short period, while immediately after the emancipation British and French influence was strong. Thus, unlike most of the Spanish-American capitals, Montevideo has little religious architecture that dates from colonial times,[16] and there are comparatively few churches of later construction.

As the nineteenth century advanced, the political fortunes of the Blancos—who traditionally received the support of the Catholic Church—declined. The new intellectual leaders—such as Varela, Rodó, and Vaz Ferreira—were liberal agnostics.[17] Batlle y Ordóñez believed that Church and State should be separated; and in religious matters, as in others, he dominated the thinking of his party.

Nevertheless, Uruguay's anti-clericals were never intolerant. When the Church was finally disestablished in 1919, it was allowed to retain its property. The calendar was purged of religious festivals: 25 December became 'Family Day', while Holy Week became an official seven days' holiday called 'Criollo Week', subsequently renamed 'Tourist Week'; but a large sum was raised by popular subscription to compensate

---

[15] Whittle, *Journal of a Voyage to the River Plate*, pp. 41 and 71.
[16] Regarding ecclesiastical architecture, see Arredondo, *Civilización del Uruguay*, i. 171–236.
[17] Cf. Arturo Ardao, 'El Liberalismo Religioso en el Uruguay', *Número* April-September 1953, pp. 138–47.

the Church for its loss of state support. Before disestablishment, however, the Church had received only very limited financial aid from the state and it had never been a direct or very powerful factor in politics. In the towns today many women are practising Catholics, and the men agnostics. There are few churches in the interior of the country, and none in the more distant villages. Religion is not taught in the state schools, but there are a number of Catholic and Protestant schools in Montevideo.

The influence of the Catholic Church on family life has been weakened not only by the impossibility of imparting religious instruction to the majority of children at school, but also by the fact that the Church marriage ceremony is not compulsory, and by the state's recognition of divorce, which is now fairly common. Divorce can be obtained by the wife at her own request, and she is not required to state her reasons for wishing to have her marriage dissolved. Batlle had hoped to arrange that divorce might equally be obtained at the will of the husband, but this proposal was rejected. It remains, however, in the Batllista programme at the present time.

In recent years the Catholic Church has attempted to increase its influence by encouraging the formation of Catholic social clubs, workers' clubs, and youth clubs. There are a number of Catholic trade unions which seem to have remained rather on the margin of the general trade union movement and which are therefore only of minor importance.

Anglican missionaries have always been allowed complete freedom to carry on their work in Uruguay. In 1845 a prosperous British business man, Samuel Lafone, built a Protestant church at Montevideo on the site of the breach by which the British invaders entered the city in 1807. William Hadfield wrote in 1854:

There is full freedom for religious worship of every kind; and Mr. Samuel Lafone, of the firm of Lafone Brothers, of Monte Video and Liverpool—a name preeminent in British trade with the Plate—having, at the expense of several thousand pounds, constructed a handsome and commodious church for the use of his Protestant fellow-countrymen, presented it, and the ground on which it stands (convenient to the anchorage for men-of-war), to them in perpetuity.[18]

---

[18] William Hadfield, *Brazil, the River Plate, and the Falkland Islands*, London, Longmans, 1854, p. 251. Protestant Lafone's marriage to an Argentine Catholic in Buenos Aires was the subject of considerable correspondence between the British and Buenos Aires governments (*cf.* H. S. Ferns, *Britain and Argentina in the Nineteenth Century*, O.U.P., 1960, pp. 237–9.)

Lafone was an admirable man. Mulhall describes him as 'one of the founders of English commerce at Montevideo.' 'He is supposed to have started the first English *saladero* [slaughter-house] and to have exported the first hides to England. He is said to have introduced the first steamer that navigated these waters, and to have built the first steam-mill. He carried on for many years an important trade with the Falkland Islands, and leased the seal-fishery at the mouth of the River Plate [i.e. the Isla de Lobos]. . . . Few men surpassed him in energy and enterprise. During a commercial crisis his house failed, but he subsequently paid all his creditors in full, besides interest. During half-a-century he held a foremost place in Montevideo.'

Humanitarian to the last, Lafone died 'attending some yellow-fever patients' at Buenos Aires in 1871. (Michael G. Mulhall, *The English in South America*, Buenos Aires, 1878, pp. 338–9).

Chapter XII

THE 1958 ELECTIONS, AND AFTER

AT the time of the elections of 1958 the Colorados had been in power for more than ninety years. In general they served the country well. In the twentieth century no Latin American country enjoyed such continuous political stability as Uruguay. The miserable shanty-towns which nowadays spread around big cities elsewhere in Latin America were not a feature of the Colorados' Montevideo. The people of Montevideo had greater opportunities for leisure than had most Latin Americans.

However, in 1958 the boom periods of the Second World War and the Korean War were long past, and the State now had difficulty in financing the benefits (such as pensions) for which the laws provided. The closing of the U.S.-owned *frigoríficos* had caused unemployment. A complex system of economic controls, taxes, and subsidies, devised and administered by a numerous bureaucracy, seemed to many to reduce the nation's ability to adapt itself to new conditions. In the late 1950's the value of the peso declined, and inflation increased faster than usual. The rural population—the creators of national wealth—still remained to a large extent outside the welfare state.

In the electoral campaign of 1958 the Colorados promised a continuation of social-welfare policies, while the Blancos naturally blamed the Colorados for the country's economic troubles and gave warning that their re-election would make matters worse.

There were, as always, subdivisions within both of the political groups, the most lively Blanco faction being the 'ruralists', whose leader, Benito Nardone, was a well-known radio commentator. For a number of years Nardone—a Montevidian by birth—had been popular among the farmers, to whom he regularly broadcast practical advice, and whom he encouraged to join together in a rural federation so that they could protect themselves against being cheated by 'city cut-throats or moneylenders'. He was scathing in his descriptions of the Colorados' ineptitude. Nardone claimed that his Rural Federation contributed 120,000 votes to the Blancos, and certainly his vigorous campaigning in the interior of the country was the final factor in bringing about the defeat of the Colorados at the polls.

At the elections of November 1958 the Blancos won 49 of the 99 seats in the Chamber of Deputies and 16 of the 31 seats in the Senate.

1959 was a fateful year. In April, when the new administration had been in office for only a few weeks, the economy suffered a further setback as the result of torrential rains, which caused the rivers in the north and west to overflow their banks, inundating about one-third of the republic, destroying crops and livestock, and flooding the hydro-electric plant at Rincón del Bonete,[1] the country's main source of electricity. While dealing with this emergency the Government prepared an economic programme that was calculated to gain the support of the International Monetary Fund. The Exchange and Monetary Reform Bill was presented to Congress in September and was promulgated shortly before the end of the year. It provided for a general easing of controls. In September also, Uruguay signed, at Montevideo, the draft of a treaty for the creation of a Latin American Free Trade Association.

The economic reform measures of 1959[2] abolished the Colorados' complex system of exchange-rates and the direct control of imports by licensing; but of course it was impossible to 'liberalize' completely and at once an economy which for so many years had been closely managed by the State. So the authorities still restricted imports by the exaction of 'prior deposits' and the imposition of 'surcharges'; and taxes on exports in the form of deductions (*detracciones*, or 'retentions')

[1] See above, p. 60.
[2] A translation of the law was published in the Foreign Information Service *Bulletin* No. 2,091 of the First National City Bank of New York, 22 December 1959.

from exchange earnings continued to be levied and were a major source of revenue.[3]

Perhaps the most beneficial undertaking during this period of Blanco rule was a campaign—backed by the United Nations Food and Agriculture Organization and the International Bank for Reconstruction and Development—to improve the quality of the country's deteriorating pasture-lands. Natural pastures in Uruguay lack protein, so that the reproduction of cattle and sheep declines. The F.A.O. recommended seeds that would provide more protein in the grass, and the World Bank offered a loan in support of a Livestock Improvement Plan. It was estimated that in two years the F.A.O.'s methods could create pastures that would be three times more productive than the natural pampa.[4]

General elections were held in November 1962, when the Blancos were again victorious, though with a reduced majority in Congress—15 senators, against the Colorados' 14; 46 deputies, against the Colorados' 45. A proposal to restore the presidential system of government, which was the subject of a national plebiscite at the same time as the elections, was defeated, so the 'collegiate' system[5] remained in force.

Uruguay experienced increasing difficulty in 1963 in financing its social services: for every 20 working people, there were 6 pensioners. In that year the attempt to maintain the peso at 11 to the U.S. dollar was abandoned, and official operations were resumed at the more realistic rate of about 16·50; towards the end of 1964 the peso was further devalued to 18·70.

Uruguay has often been referred to as the Switzerland or the Sweden of South America. Nevertheless, when you travel by rutted earth roads across the shimmering but rather desolate pasture-lands; among the grassy hills, with their granite outcrops; over the northern plains that are dotted with tall,

---

[3] *Quarterly Review*, Bank of London & South America, October 1960, pp. 77–8.
[4] *New York Times*, International Edition, Latin American Economic Review, 17 January 1962.   [5] See above, pp. 37–9.

H

tufted palm-trees standing isolated in the sun—you know that this country is quite different from anything European. The winds that blow across Uruguay, bending the silvery grass, come from over the vast flatness of the Argentine pampa; and the sun is the sub-tropical sun of Brazil. The republic's wealth is in the roaming multitudes of sheep and cattle—and in the rough horsemen who treat them with so little respect. You are impressed by the 'backwardness' of these vital, wealth-giving rural regions: the lonely shacks that serve as dwellings for the herdsmen on the open grazing-lands; the sad villages that are the colour of the brown earth of which they are made; the *terutero* birds uttering their unhappy cry; the solitary owls, dazzled by the daylight, squatting on the fence-posts; the violent rainstorms—you recognize that this is still the Uruguay described by Charles Darwin and W. H. Hudson. All the more remarkable, then, that such a remote outpost should have produced in the nineteenth century men of such enlightenment as Varela, Rodó, and Batlle, and that the nation —in so far as Montevideo is the nation—should have been moulded by their teaching. When you travel through the interior, you are reminded that the appearance of most of the land and the life of the people who inhabit it have not changed so very greatly since the days of the civil wars, when the rival gangs of horsemen galloped over these same hills and plains. Uruguay's tradition of orderly and progressive government is barely fifty years old.

This welfare state differs from the European models not only in appearance, but in character. As Lord Bryce wrote, the nation has retained something of the gaucho's breezy recklessness and audacity. Perhaps (as many Uruguayans believe) social legislation has been pushed ahead too fast and too far. Simon G. Hanson remarked of one of the labour laws that it was 'idealistic, impracticable, difficult to enforce' and therefore 'characteristically Uruguayan'.[6] Under the 'collegiate' form of government there have been prolonged disputes within the ruling party, and procrastination.

But Batlle himself was a sort of urban gaucho, and Uruguay is still basically a gaucho's welfare state, rather capricious in the management of its affairs.

[6] *Utopia in Uruguay*, p. 130.

APPENDICES

I. PRODUCTION OF LIVESTOCK AND WHEAT

Head of Cattle (million)		Sheep (million)	
1951	8·3	Before Second	
1956	7·42	World War	18
1961	8·67	1956	23·3
		1961	21·48

Source: Bank of London & South America

Wheat

	Area (hectares)	Production (metric tons)
1946–7	371,358	181,826
1947–8	504,947	423,542
1948–9	517,990	518,301
1949–50	516,489	451,976
1950–1	495,661	434,729
1951–2	583,902	477,588
1952–3	513,936	462,525
1953–4	747,878	818,619
1954–5	771,589	853,572
1955–6	819,466	876,181
1956–7	688,488	588,891
1957–8	777,945	597,763
1958–9	690,749	359,703
1959–60	293,323	182,832*
1960–1	531,500	445,405

* This was the year of the floods. See above, p. 104

Source: Banco de la República

II. BALANCE OF TRADE, 1946–63

Million U.S. $

	Exports f.o.b.	*Imports c.i.f.*	*Balance*
1946	152·8	147·2	+ 5·6
1947	162·5	215·1	− 52·6
1948	177·7	200·4	− 22·7
1949	191·6	181·2	+ 10·4
1950	254·3	200·8	+ 53·5
1951	236·3	309·4	− 73·1
1952	208·8	236·6	− 27·8
1953	269·5	193·1	+ 76·4
1954	248·9	273·2	− 24·3
1955	183·7	225·0	− 41·3
1956	211·1	205·8	+ 5·3
1957	128·1	226·4	− 98·3
1958	138·6	134·6	+ 4·0
1959	97·8	214·0	−116·2
1960	129·4	228·6	− 99·2
1961	174·7	207·6	− 32·8
1962	153·4	229·9	− 76·5
1963	165·2	176·8	− 11·7

BALANCE OF TRADE WITH U.K. & U.S.A., 1958–63

	1958	*1959*	*1960*	*1961*	*1962*	*1963*
United Kingdom	+13·0	+ 2·5	+11·7	+20·9	+ 1·9	+17·8
United States	− 5·8	−20·5	−45·6	−23·2	−20·1	− 8·8

Source: Bank of London & South America

III. EXPORTS AND IMPORTS

1. Exports: Direction of Trade
Million U.S. $

	1961	*1962*	*1963*
EXPORTS—Total	*174·7*	*153·4*	*165·2*
AREAS			
U.S.A. and Canada	25·5	24·4	19·1
Latin America	6·3	9·1	15·7
LAFTA	*5·8*	*8·0*	*15·0*
Continental Europe	77·6	65·3	69·2
EEC	*63·2*	*52·9*	*53·6*
Sterling Area	45·1	27·7	42·5
Soviet Area	14·9	24·2	11·2
COUNTRIES			
United Kingdom	42·2	25·0	39·3
Netherlands	20·0	15·3	18·6
U.S.A.	23·8	23·7	18·5
Western Germany	14·9	15·2	12·1
Italy	11·8	8·0	10·7
Brazil	1·8	3·0	9·7
France	10·9	8·4	8·1
Japan	4·0	1·0	5·2
Sweden	1·6	3·1	4·7
Spain	5·3	3·0	4·5
Belgium	5·7	6·1	4·2
U.S.S.R.	0·9	12·8	3·8
Czechoslovakia	4·8	3·8	3·6
Others	27·0	25·0	22·2

III. EXPORTS AND IMPORTS—*continued*

2. *Exports: Commodity Composition*
Million U.S. $

	1961	1962	1963
EXPORTS—Total	174·7	153·4	165·2
Wool, raw	85·6	58·3	58·4
Greasy	73·6	49·8	50·0
Washed	12·0	8·6	8·4
Meat and meat products	27·4	31·4	33·4
Beef	24·0	27·9	29·7
Wool Tops, combed	24·3	23·3	26·6
Hides and skins	16·8	17·3	17·6
Cattle hides	8·3	9·7	8·3
Sheep skins	7·6	6·7	8·2
Linseed oil	6·5	4·1	6·1
Other exports	13·3	19·0	23·1
DESTINATIONS			
Wool, raw:	85·6	58·3	58·4
United Kingdom	29·7	13·6	21·3
U.S.A.	13·8	11·5	7·8
Western Germany	6·3	5·7	4·8
Japan	3·6	2·9	4·4
Meat and meat products:	27·4	31·4	33·4
United Kingdom	9·7	8·6	14·5
U.S.A.	5·5	5·8	5·6
Wool tops, combed:	24·3	23·3	26·6
Netherlands	9·5	8·3	9·4
Italy	5·4	3·4	3·9

Source: Bank of London & South America

III. EXPORTS AND IMPORTS—*continued*

3. Imports: Direction of Trade

Million U.S. $

	1961	*1962*	*1963*
IMPORTS—Total	*207·6*	*229·9*	*176·8*
AREAS			
U.S.A. and Canada	49·5	47·2	30·5
Latin America	47·5	46·8	45·3
LAFTA	*34·5*	*34·0*	*31·7*
Continental Europe	65·0	83·1	55·5
EEC	*52·6*	*64·2*	*41·9*
Sterling Area	25·7	29·8	26·0
Soviet Area	4·1	3·0	1·9
COUNTRIES			
U.S.A.	46·9	43·9	27·3
United Kingdom	21·4	23·2	21·5
Western Germany	25·9	31·5	18·3
Brazil	17·5	20·5	13·9
Arabia	7·2	12·6	10·4
France	7·9	11·8	9·7
Argentina	11·9	8·6	9·6
Venezuela	12·0	10·6	8·7
Italy	9·2	10·1	7·6
Cuba	0·8	1·8	4·8
Japan	1·4	3·4	4·2
Belgium	5·1	7·4	3·5
Sweden	3·9	5·1	3·4
Canada	2·6	3·3	3·2
Others	33·9	36·1	30·7

III. EXPORTS AND IMPORTS—*continued*

4. *Imports: Commodity Composition*
Million U.S. $

	1961	*1962*	*1963*
IMPORTS—*Total*	207·6	229·9	176·8
Raw materials	71·0	66·0	57·6
Sugar, raw	*8·1*	*4·3*	*8·1*
Cotton, raw	*5·7*	*3·4*	*3·4*
Newsprint	*3·8*	*3·8*	*3·2*
Tobacco, raw	*4·4*	*5·6*	*3·1*
Vehicles and parts	33·3	41·1	30·6
Machinery, apparatus	21·8	34·1	25·7
Fuels and lubricants	26·8	30·3	24·7
Petroleum, crude	*21·0*	*24·5*	*20·7*
Construction materials	11·0	9·9	6·2
Timber, structural	*4·8*	*4·9*	*3·3*
Pharmaceutical products	3·9	4·9	4·5
Electrical apparatus	6·2	6·2	3·6
Radio, photo. equipment	7·7	8·6	2·4
Other imports	25·7	28·8	21·5
SOURCES			
Raw materials:	71·0	66·0	57·6
U.S.A.	*15·3*	*10·8*	*7·7*
Brazil	*8·5*	*8·3*	*6·3*
Western Germany	*7·0*	*6·8*	*6·3*
Vehicles and parts:	33·3	41·1	30·6
United Kingdom	*10·4*	*11·7*	*13·3*
U.S.A.	*9·8*	*8·4*	*4·7*
Western Germany	*8·2*	*11·2*	*4·5*
Machinery, apparatus:	21·8	34·1	25·7
U.S.A.	*7·6*	*10·6*	*7·2*
Fuels and lubricants:	26·8	30·3	24·7
Arabia	*7·2*	*12·6*	*10·4*

Source: Bank of London & South America

BIBLIOGRAPHY

I. LATIN AMERICA: GENERAL

Benham, F., and Holley, H. A. *The Economy of Latin America*. Oxford University Press, R.I.I.A., 1960.

Cady, J. F. *Foreign Intervention in the Rio de la Plata*. University of Pennsylvania Press, 1929.

Chevalier, Pierre, *Histoire de l'Amérique Latine*. Paris, Presses Universitaires de France (Que sais-je? series).

Davies, Howell (ed.) *The South American Handbook*. London, Trade and Travel Publications, (published yearly, Sept. 29, 1921, being useful information for travellers).

Dozer, Donald Marquand. *Latin America: An Interpretive History*. 1962.

Humphreys, R. A. *The Evolution of Modern Latin America*. Oxford, 1946.

Martin, P. A. *Latin America and the War*. Baltimore, Johns Hopkins Press, 1925.

—————— *The Republics of Latin America*. New York, Oxford University Press, 1950.

Great Britain, Ministry of Agriculture and Fisheries, Economic Advisory Council, Agricultural Marketing Report (annual) A. and A.S. *Annual Report*, 1930.

Martin, C. E. *The Latin American Republics*. (Second ed.) 1920, Ginn Press, 1947.

Herring, Hubert. *A History of Latin America*. Knopf, annual supplement.

BIBLIOGRAPHY

I. LATIN AMERICA: GENERAL

Benham, F., and Holley, H. A. *The Economy of Latin America*. London, Oxford University Press for R.I.I.A., 1960.

Cady, J. F. *Foreign Intervention in the Rio de la Plata, 1838–50*. University of Pennsylvania Press, 1929.

Chaunu, Pierre. *Histoire de l'Amérique Latine*. Paris, Presses Universitaires de France ('Que sais-je?' series), 1949.

Davies, Howell, ed. *The South American Handbook*. London, Trade and Travel Publications. (Published annually. Contains useful information for travellers.)

DeConde, Alexander. *Herbert Hoover's Latin-American Policy*. California, Stanford University, 1951.

Fitzgibbon, R. H., ed. *The Constitutions of the Americas*. University of Chicago Press, 1948.

García Calderón, F. *Latin America: its Rise and Progress*, trans. by Bernard Miall. 7th ed. London, Fisher Unwin, 1924. (First published 1913.)

Gordon, Wendell, G. *The Economy of Latin America*. New York, Columbia University Press, 1950.

Great Britain, Ministry of Agriculture and Fisheries. *Report of the South American Agricultural Mission, 1947*. London, 1947, mimeo.

Hanke, Lewis. *South America*. Princeton, N.J., Van Nostrand (Anvil Series), 1959.

Haring, C. H. *The Spanish Empire in America*. New York, Oxford University Press, 1947.

Herring, Hubert. *A History of Latin America*. London, Cape, 1956.

Hughlett, Lloyd J., ed. *Industrialization in Latin America*. New York, McGraw-Hill, 1946.

Humphreys, R. A. *British Consular Reports on the Trade and Politics of Latin America, 1824–6*. London, Royal Historical Society, 1940. (Camden 3rd Ser., vol. 63.)

—— *The Evolution of Modern Latin America*. Oxford, Clarendon Press, 1946.

—— *Latin American History: A Guide to the Literature in English*. London, Oxford University Press for R.I.I.A., 1958.

James, Preston E. *Latin America*. Rev. ed. New York, Odyssey Press, 1950.

Jorrín, Miguel. *Governments of Latin America*. New York, Van Nostrand, 1953.

Kirkpatrick, F. A. *Latin America: a Brief History*. Cambridge University Press, 1938.

Lynch, John. *Spanish Colonial Administration, 1782–1810*. University of London, Athlone Press, 1958.

Macdonald, Austin F. *Latin American Politics and Government*. New York, Crowell, 1949.

Manchester, A. K. *British Preëminence in Brazil: its Rise and Decline*, University of North Carolina Press, 1933. (Includes the history of the relations between Brazil and Uruguay.)

Martin, Percy A. *Latin America and the War*. Baltimore, Johns Hopkins University Press, 1925.

Mulhall, Michael G. *The English in South America*. Buenos Aires, 'The Standard', 1878.

Rippy, J. Fred. *Historical Evolution of Latin America*. 3rd ed. New York, Crofts, 1945.

—— *Latin America and the Industrial Age*. New York, Putnam, 1944.

Robertson, William Spence. *France and Latin American Independence*. Baltimore, Johns Hopkins Press, 1939.

Sánchez, Luis Alberto. *Existe América Latina?* Mexico, Fondo de Cultura Económica, 1945.

Schurz, William Lytle. *This New World: the Civilization of Latin America*. London, Allen and Unwin, 1956.

United Nations:

    Dept. of Economic Affairs. *Foreign Capital in Latin America*. New York, 1955.

    Dept. of Economic Affairs. *Study of Trade between Latin America and Europe*. Geneva, 1953. (Prepared by the Secretariat of the Economic Commission for Latin America, the Economic Commission for Europe, and the Food and Agriculture Organization.)

ECLA. *Economic Survey of Latin America.* (Annually.)

Webster, C. K. *Britain and the Independence of Latin America, 1812–1830.* 2 vols. Oxford University Press, for the Ibero-American Institute of Great Britain, 1938.

Who's Who in Latin America: Pt. V. (Argentina, Paraguay, and Uruguay.) California, Stanford University, 1950.

Worcester, Donald E., and Schaeffer, Wendell G. *The Growth and Culture of Latin America.* New York, Oxford University Press, 1956.

Wythe, George. *Industry in Latin America.* 2nd ed. New York, Columbia University Press, 1949.

II. URUGUAY: GENERAL

(History, Economy, &c.)

Acevedo, Eduardo. *Anales históricos del Uruguay.* 5 vols. Montevideo, 1933–4.

—— *José Artigas: Su obra cívica.* 2nd ed. Montevideo, 1933.

—— *Manuel de historia uruguaya: desde el coloniaje hasta 1930.* Montevideo, 1935.

—— *Manual de historia uruguaya: Artigas.* 3rd ed. Montevideo, 1942.

—— *Manual de historia uruguaya: después de Artigas.* 3rd ed. Montevideo, 1943.

Aguiar, José. *Nuestra frontera con el Brasil.* Montevideo, 1936.

Amézaga, José. *Uruguay y el Brasil.* Montevideo, 1942.

Anon. *Nouveaux rapports sur les colonies agricoles suisses en Uruguay.* Bale, Krüsi, 1861. (Colonia Suiza, near the town of Colonia, is still famous for its dairy farming, cheeses, &c.)

Arcas, José Antonio. *Historia del siglo XX uruguayo (1897–1943).* Montevideo, 1950.

Arena, Domingo. *Batlle y los problemas sociales del Uruguay.* Montevideo, 1937.

Azarola Gil, Luis Enrique. *Las Orígenes de Montevideo.* Montevideo, 1933.

Barbagelata, Lorenzo. *Artigas antes de 1810.* Montevideo, 1945.

Bauzá, Francisco. *Historia de la dominación española en el Uruguay.* 3rd ed. Montevideo, 1929.

Blanco Acevedo, Pablo. *Centenario de la independencia.* 2nd ed. Montevideo, 1940.

—— *El federalismo de Artigas y la independencia nacional.* Montevideo, 1939.

—— *El gobierno colonial en el Uruguay y los orígenes de la nacionalidad.* 3rd ed. Montevideo, 1944.

—— *Estudios constitucionales.* Montevideo, 1939.

Buero, Juan Antonio. *El Uruguay en la vida international.* Montevideo, 1919.

Castaing, M. P. *Uruguay: Monographie.* Montevideo, 1949.

Chiarino, J. Vicente and Miguel Saralegui. *Detrás de la Ciudad.* Montevideo, 1944.

Consejo Interamericano de Comercio y Producción. *Encuesta continental sobre fomento y coordinación de industrias, respuesta referente a la República Oriental del Uruguay.* 2nd ed. Montevideo, 1947.

—— *Uruguay y el Plan Marshall.* Montevideo, 1948.

Cosco Montaldo, Oscar. *El Uruguay, su democracia y su vida política.* Montevideo, 1926.

Cosio, Pedro. *El proceso de la crisis de 1929 y 1931.* Montevideo. (No date.)

—— *Las defensas economicas contra la gran depresión.* Montevideo, 1936.

Couture, Eduardo J. *La Constitution uruguayenne de 1952.* Paris, Extrait des Cahiers de Législation et de Bibliographie Juridique de l'Amérique Latine, Nos. 11–12. (The text of the 1952 Constitution in French, preceded by an authoritative commentary.)

Couture, Eduardo J., and others. *Legislatión vigente en el Uruguay.* Montevideo, Facultad de Derecho y Ciencias Sociales, 1956. (A summary of Uruguayan legislation.)

De-María, Isidoro. *Hombres notables de la República Oriental del Uruguay,* ed. by J. E. Pivel Devoto. Montevideo, 1939.

Dumas, Alexandre. *Montevideo, ou une nouvelle Troi.* Paris, 1850.

Duprey, Jacques. *Voyage aux origines françaises de l'Uruguay.* Montevideo, Instituto Histórico y Geografico del Uruguay, 1952. (The standard work on the French contribution to the country's development. Interesting illustrations.)

Falcão Espalter, Mario. *Formación histórica del Uruguay.* Madrid, 1929.

Faraone, Roque. *La Prensa de Montevideo.* Montevideo, Facultad de Derecho, 1960.

Fernández Saldaña, José M. *Diccionario uruguayo de biografías, 1810–1940.* Montevideo, 1945.

Ferreiro, Felipe. *Orígenes uruguayos.* Montevideo, 1937.

Fitzgibbon, Russell H. *Uruguay: Portrait of a Democracy.* New Brunswick, Rutgers University Press, 1954. London, Allen & Unwin, 1956. (A comprehensive and enthusiastic volume.)

Freitas, Newton. *Garibaldi en América.* Buenos Aires, Editorial Nova, 1946. (Colección Mar Dulce.)

Gandía, Enrique de. *Los treinta y tres orientales y la independencia del Uruguay.* Buenos Aires, 1939.

Gilles, Albert. *L'Uruguay, pays heureux*. Preface by André Maurois. Paris, Nouvelles Editions Latines, 1952.

Giudici, Roberto B. *Battle y el Batllismo*. Montevideo, 1928.

—— *Los Fundamentos del Batllismo*. 2nd ed. Montevideo, 1947.

Giuffra, Elzear S. *La República del Uruguay: explicación geográfica del territorio nacional*. Montevideo, 1935.

Glanville, B., and Weinstein, J. *World Cup*, London, Hale, 1958. (World football, with some references to Uruguay's part in it.)

Gómez Haedo, Juan Carlos. *Relaciones de Inglaterra con los países del Plata: su influencia en el Uruguay*. Montevideo, 1939.

González, Ariosto D., and others. *Artigas: homenaje en el centenario de su muerte*. Montevideo, Instituto Histórico y Geográfico del Uruguay, 1952.

—— *Iconografía de Montevideo*, Concejo Departmental de Montevideo, 1955.

Great Britain:

Board of Trade. *Hints to Business Men Visiting Uruguay*. London, 1961. (A pamphlet.)

Commercial Relations and Export Dept. *Uruguay: Economic and Social Conditions*, by C. B. B. Heathcote-Smith. London, H.M.S.O., 1954. (Overseas Economic Surveys.)

Ministry of Agriculture and Fisheries. *Report of the South American Agricultural Mission*. London, H.M.S.O., 1947.

Güinasso, Luis María. *Uruguay: tibia Arcadia*. Montevideo, 1945.

Hanson, Simon G. *Utopia in Uruguay: Chapters in the Economic History of Uruguay*. New York, Oxford University Press, 1938.

—— *Argentine Meat and the British Market*. California, Stanford University Press, 1938.

Herrera, Luis Alberto de. *El Uruguay internacional*. Paris, 1912.

—— *La Misión Ponsonby*. Montevideo, 1930.

—— *La Paz de 1828*. Montevideo, 1938.

Instituto de Investigaciones Geográficas. *El Suelo del Uruguay*. Montevideo, 1948.

Jiménez de Aréchaga, Justino. *Panorama institucional del Uruguay a mediados del siglo XX*. Montevideo, 1949.

Lasplaces, Alberto. *Vida admirable de José Pedro Varela*, 2nd ed. Montevideo, 1944. (A life of the educational reformer.)

Martínez Lamas, Julio. *Economia uruguaya*. Montevideo, 1943.

—— *Riqueza y pobreza del Uruguay*. 2nd ed. Montevideo, 1946. (A study of the conflicting interests of Montevideo and the rural districts.)

Mora Otero, José A. *Sentido internacional del Uruguay*. Montevideo, 1938.

Narancio, Edmundo M. and Federico Capurro Calamet. *Historia y análisis estadístico de la población.* Montevideo, 1939.

Otaegui, Tomás. *Los Vascos en el Uruguay.* Buenos Aires, 1943.

Pan American Union. *Uruguay.* Washington, 1954. (An illustrated pamphlet, useful for foreign visitors.)

Petit Muñoz, Eugenio, with Edmundo M. Narancio and José M. Traibel Nelcis. *La condición de los negros durante el coloniaje.* Montevideo, 1947.

Pintos, Francisco R. *Batlle y el proceso histórico del Uruguay.* Montevideo, 1942.

Pivel Devoto, Juan E. *Historia de los partidos políticos en el Uruguay.* Montevideo, 1942.

—— and Alcira Ranieri de Pivel Devoto. *Historia de la República Oriental del Uruguay.* Montevideo, 1945.

Riva-Zucchelli, Pedro, *Historia de la independencia de la República Oriental.* Montevideo, 1934.

Rodríguez Fabregat, E. *Batlle y Ordóñez.* Buenos Aires, 1942.

Rodríguez Larreta, Eduardo and others. *El aporte de Inglaterra a la civilización occidental.* Montevideo, 1940.

Salgado, José. *El federalismo de Artigas.* Montevideo, 1945.

—— *Historia diplomática de la independencia oriental.* Montevideo, 1945.

Sanguinetti Freire, Alberto. *Legislación social del Uruguay.* 2 vols. 2nd ed. Montevideo, 1949.

Silva Vila, Juan. *Ideario de Artigas.* Montevideo, 1942.

Street, John. *Artigas and the Emancipation of Uruguay.* London, Oxford University Press, 1959.

Traibel, José María. *Breviario Artiguista.* Montevideo, Colombino, 1951.

United States Tariff Commission. *Economic Controls and Commercial Policy in Uruguay.* Washington, U.S.G.P.O., 1945.

—— *Mining and Manufacturing Industries in Uruguay.* Washington, U.S.G.P.O., 1945. Reprinted 1949.

Wirth, Juan Carlos F. *Colonia Suiza hace ochenta años: la inmigración al Uruguay en 1861.* Montevideo, 1944.

Ysita, Eugene, ed. *National Economy of Uruguay, 1941–1946,* Part I, Washington, Pan American Union, 1948. (Commercial Pan American series No. 179.)

Zabaleta, Roberto, and others. *El Contralor de las importaciones y exportaciones en el Uruguay.* Montevideo, Mosca, 1954.

Zorilla de San Martín, Juan. *La epopeya de Artigas.* 2 vols. 2nd ed. Barcelona, 1916.

Zum Felde, Alberto. *Evolución histórica del Uruguay.* 3rd ed. Montevideo, 1945.

III. EARLY TRAVEL AND DESCRIPTION

Beaumont, J. A. B. *Travels in Buenos Ayres and the Adjacent Country.* . . . London, Ridgway, 1828.

Darwin, Charles. *The Voyage of the Beagle.* First published in 1839. (See also Darwin's original diary of the voyage, edited by Nora Barlow, published by the Cambridge University Press, 1933.)

Davie, John Constanse. *Letters from Paraguay.* London, Robinson, 1805. (A visitor to Montevideo in 1797.)

Gregory, William. *A Visible Display of Divine Providence; or, The Journal of a Captured Missionary.* . . . 2nd ed. London, 1801.

Howell, William. *Some Interesting Particulars of the Second Voyage made by the Missionary Ship, the 'Duff'.* . . . Knaresborough, Hargrove, 1809.

Isabelle, Arsène. *Voyage à Buenos-Ayres.* . . . Havre, J. Morlent, 1835.

Jones, Tom B. *South America Rediscovered.* University of Minnesota, 1949 (quoting early nineteenth-century travellers).

Mackinnon, Commander. *Steam Warfare in the Parana.* . . . 2 vols. London, Charles Ollier, 1848.

Mawe, John. *Travels in the Gold and Diamond Districts of Brazil.* London, Longmans, 1825. (Contains descriptions of the interior of the Banda Oriental.)

Robertson, J. and W. P. Parish. *Letters on Paraguay.* . . 3 vols. London, Murray, 1838 and 1839.

Scarlett, the Hon. P. Campbell. *South America and the Pacific.* . . . 2 vols. London, Henry Colburn, 1838.

Vidal, E. E. *Picturesque Illustrations of Buenos Ayres and Monte Video.* London, Ackermann, 1820. (A beautifully illustrated volume.)

Wafer, Lionel. *A New Voyage and Description of the Isthmus of America,* ed. L. E. Elliott Joyce. Oxford, Hakluyt Society, 1934.

Webster, W. H. B. *Narrative of a Voyage to the Southern Atlantic Ocean.* . . . 2 vols. London, Richard Bentley, 1834.

Whittle, W. *Journal of a Voyage to the River Plate.* . . . Manchester, Bradshawe & Blacklock, 1846.

IV. LATER TRAVEL AND DESCRIPTION

Bryce, James. *South America: Observations and Impressions.* New York, Macmillan, 1912.

Burton, Richard F. *Letters from the Battle-fields of Paraguay.* London, Tinsley, 1870.

Crawford, Robert. *Across the Pampas and the Andes.* London, Longmans, 1884.

Forbes, Rosita. *Eight Republics in Search of a Future*. London, Cassell, 1933. (Superficial, but vivid. The author had helpful personal connexions with Uruguay.)

Frank, Waldo. *South American Journey*. London, Gollancz, 1944.

Hadfield, William. *Brazil, the River Plate and the Falkland Islands*. London, Longmans, 1854.

Hudson, W. H. *The Purple Land*. First published in 1885. (A partly autobiographical novel.)

Koebel, W. H. *The Great South Land*. London, Thornton Butterworth, 1919.

—— *Uruguay*. London, T. Fisher Unwin, 1911.

Latham, William. *The States of the River Plate: Their Industries and Commerce*. London, Longmans, 1866.

Mikes, George. *Tango*. London, Deutsch, 1961. (A travel book by a humourist who has a flair for pointing out national idiosyncracies. 'Montevideo', he writes, 'is full of charming, cultured, cynical intellectuals who, instead of beating their chests and trying to overwhelm you with statistics and spurious facts, take a special and sophisticated pleasure in deriding their charming, tiny and slightly provincial country. One writer said: "Our great strength is that we have no oil, no minerals, nothing. We are so pleased. They are searching for oil now. I hope that they will not find any." ' The nearest that Mikes could get to the truth about Uruguay's economic situation was the comment of another Uruguayan, who explained, with apparent unconcern: 'We are very advanced as consumers, but rather backward as producers.')

Mulhall, M. G. and E. T. *Handbook of the River Plate*. 6th ed. Buenos Aires, 1892.

Murray, J. H. *Travels in Uruguay*. . . . London, Longmans, 1871.

Orden, Ernesto La. *Uruguay, el Benjamín de España*. Madrid, 1949.

Pritchett, V. S. 'South America'. in *Holiday*, Philadelphia, November 1956. (Pritchett comments humourously on the 'collegiate' system of government in force at the time of his visit to Uruguay. The National Council of Government, he explains, consists of nine members, six of whom come from the leading political group and three from the next, and this ratio is observed in the making of appointments in various branches of the administration. In Pritchett's words: 'A Committee of Nine, representing the two political groups, runs the country—their nine Cadillacs stand outside the Presidential Palace. So well regulated are the Uruguayans, so caught by the prosaic magic of fair shares, that even the jobs in many state organizations are distributed proportionately to the two political groups. If nine stevedores are required on the docks, they must be in the correct party proportions of six to three. This making of everything go by nines is a religion.' Of course Pritchett exaggerates.)

Ross, Gordon, *Argentina and Uruguay*. London, Methuen, 1917.

V. THE ENGLISH INVASIONS (1806–7)

Anon. *An Authentic Narrative of the Proceedings of the Expedition under the Command of Brigadier-Gen. Crawfurd.* . . . London, 1808.

Fortescue, the Hon. J. W. *The History of the British Army*. Vol. v. London, Macmillan, 1910. (Contains an account of the British invasions of the River Plate, 1806–7.)

González, Ariosto D., ed. *The Southern Star: La Estrella del Sur*. Montevideo, Instituto Histórico y Geográfico del Uruguay, 1942. (Complete reproduction, in facsimile, of the newspaper published during the British occupation of Montevideo, 1807.)

Parkinson, C. Northcote, ed. *Samuel Walters, Lieutenant R.N.: His Memoirs*. Liverpool University Press, 1949. (Walters's sketch-maps of Maldonado will be of interest to modern visitors to the fashionable seaside resort of Punta del Este.)

[Pococke, Captain.] *Journal of a Soldier of the 71st, or Glasgow Regiment.* . . . 2nd ed. Edinburgh, Tait & Black, 1819.

Roberts, Carlos. *Las invasiones inglesas.* . . . Buenos Aires, Peuser, 1938.

[Watson, George.] *A Narrative of the Adventures of a Greenwich Pensioner*. Newcastle, 1827.

VI. THE BATTLE OF THE RIVER PLATE (1939)

Campbell, Commander A. B. *The Battle of the River Plate*. London, Jenkins, 1940.

Guani, Alberto. *Antecedentes relativos al hundimiento del acorazado 'Admiral Graf Spee'*. Montevideo, 1940.

Pope, Dudley. *The Battle of the River Plate*. London, Kimber, 1956.

Powell, Michael. *Graf Spee*. London, Hodder & Stoughton, 1956. (The author, with Emeric Pressburger, produced the film of the Battle of the River Plate, which was chosen for the Royal Command Performance, London, 1956.)

Rasenack, F. W. *La Batalla del Río de la Plata*. Buenos Aires, Gure, 1957. (An account, in diary form, of the Battle of the River Plate by the fire-control officer in the German 'pocket battle-ship' *Graf Spee*.)

VII. CULTURE

Ardao, Arturo. *Batlle y Ordóñez y el positivismo filosófico*. Montevideo, Número, 1951.

—— *Espiritualismo y positivismo en el Uruguay*. Mexico, Fondo de Cultura Económica, 1950. (Colección Tierra Firme.)

—— *Filosofía pre-universitaria en el Uruguay*. Montevideo, Claudio García, 1945. (Biblioteca Rodó.)

Argul, José Pedro. *El pintor José Cúneo, paisajista del Uruguay*. Montevideo, Editorial San Felipe y Santiago, 1949. (An illustrated study of the artist's work.)

Arredondo, Horacio. *Civilización del Uruguay: aspectos arqueológicos y sociológicos 1600–1900*. Preface by Ariosto D. González. 2 vols. Montevideo, Instituto Histórico y Geográfico del Uruguay, 1951. (The standard iconography. Profusely illustrated.)

Crawford, W. R. *A Century of Latin American Thought*. Cambridge, Harvard University Press, 1945.

Etcheverry, José Enrique, and others. *Revista del Instituto Nacional de Investigaciones y Archivos Literarios*. Montevideo, 1949. (Essays in literary history.)

Henríquez-Ureña, Pedro. *Literary Currents in Hispanic America*. Cambridge, Harvard University Press, 1949. (The best book on the subject.)

Herrera MacLean, Carlos A. *Pedro Figari*. Buenos Aires, Poseidon, 1943. (Contains reproductions of many of Figari's paintings.)

Hespelt, E. Herman, ed. *An Outline of Spanish American Literature*. 2nd ed. New York, Crofts, 1947.

Museo Histórico Nacional. *Catálogo descriptivo. I. Historia general de la República*. Montevideo, 1946. (A comprehensive, illustrated catalogue of the Museum, directed by Juan E. Pivel Devoto.)

Otero, Gustavo Adolfo. *La cultura y el periodismo*. 2nd ed. Quito (Ecuador), Liebmann, 1953.

Podestá, José María. *J. Torres García*. Buenos Aires, Losada, 1946. (Photographs of the artist's work.)

Rodríguez Monegal, Emir. *José E. Rodó en el novecientos*. Montevideo, Número, 1950.

Torre Revello, José, *Contribución a la historia y bibliografía en Montevideo*. Buenos Aires, Facultad de Filosofía y Letras, 1926.

—— *Historia de mi vida*. Montevideo, Asociación de Arte Constructivo, 1939 (Autobiography of the artist.)

Zani, Giselda. *Pedro Figari*. Buenos Aires, Losada, 1944. (Photographs of Figari's paintings.)

Zum Felde, Alberto. *Indice crítico de la literatura hispanoamericana: la ensayística.* Mexico, Editorial Guaranía, 1954. (An encyclopaedic work by Uruguay's leading literary historian. Reference to Uruguayan authors are of particular interest.)

—— *Proceso intelectual del Uruguay.* Montevideo, 1930.

VIII. PERIODICALS

Fortnightly Review and *Quarterly Review*, London, Bank of London & South America.

Hispanic American Historical Review, Durham (N.C.), Duke University Press (quarterly).

Hispanic American Report, California, Stanford University. (A monthly review of current affairs.)

Inter-American Economic Affairs, Washington, Institute of Inter-American Studies (quarterly).

Marcha, Montevideo. (An independent weekly. Politics, economics, and the arts.)

New York Times. As Latin America is largely ignored by British newspapers—except when a dictator is overthrown or an earthquake devastates some Andean region—those of us living in the United Kingdom who wish to keep up to date with Latin American affairs rely to a considerable extent on the international edition of the *New York Times*, published daily in Europe.

Número, Montevideo. (A distinguished literary review published at irregular intervals from 1949 to 1955.)

Uruguay, Banco de la República, Departamento de Investigaciones Económicas, *Revista* (quarterly) and *Suplemento Estadístico de la Revista Económica* (monthly).

IX. ADDENDA

Jesualdo [Jesualdo Sosa]. *Artigas, del vasallaje a la revolución.* Buenos Aires, Losada, 1961. (A biography of the national hero by an Uruguayan author.)

Joslin, David. *A Century of Banking in Latin America.* Oxford University Press, 1963. (Many references to British banking, investment, and trade in Uruguay.)

Lindahl, Göran G. *Uruguay's New Path: a Study of Politics during the First Colegiado, 1919–33.* Stockholm, Institute of Ibero-American Studies, 1962.

Maggi, Carlos. *El Uruguay y su gente*. Montevideo, Alfa,1963. (An amusing, penetrating, and very Uruguayan commentary. 'We only recognize the greatness of our country when we make a little journey by bicycle.')

Millington-Drake, Sir Eugen. *The Drama of Graf Spee and the Battle of the Plate*. London, Peter Davies, 1964. (An anthology of naval and other documents, and reminiscences, compiled by the charming man who was British Minister to Uruguay at the time of the battle, in 1939.)

Real de Azúa, Carlos. 'Batlle y su época', a reappraisal of Batlle y Ordóñez published in three instalments in *Marcha*, 10, 17, and 24 May 1963.

Vanger, Milton I. *José Batlle y Ordóñez: the creator of his times*. Harvard University Press, 1963. (In this book Professor Vanger deals with Batlle's rise to power and first presidency. A volume on Batlle's second presidency is in preparation.)

INDEX

*Set at The Broadwater Press
Welwyn Garden City, Herts
and reprinted lithographically
by Latimer Trend & Co. Ltd.,
Plymouth and Whitstable*